Science and Math Explorations for Young Children

A GEMS / PEACHES Handbook for Early Childhood Educators, Childcare Providers, and Parents

by
Katharine Barrett, Ellen Blinderman,
Beatrice Boffen, Jean Echols, Patricia A. House,
Kimi Hosoume, Jaine Kopp

with contributions from
Carl Babcock, Lincoln Bergman

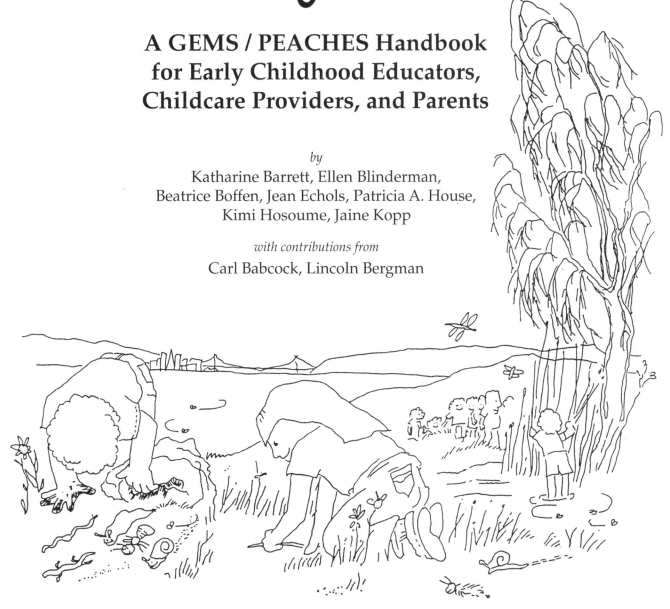

Lawrence Hall of Science
University of California at Berkeley

The Lawrence Hall of Science (LHS) is a public science center on the University of California at Berkeley campus. LHS offers a full program of activities for the public. LHS is also a center for teacher education and curriculum research and development.

Initial support for the origination and publication of the GEMS series was provided by the A.W. Mellon Foundation and the Carnegie Corporation of New York. Under a grant from the National Science Foundation, GEMS Leader's Workshops have been held across the country. GEMS has also received support from the McDonnell-Douglas Foundation and the McDonnell-Douglas Employee's Community Fund; the Employees Community Fund of Boeing California and the Boeing Corporation; the Hewlett Packard Company; the people at Chevron USA; the William K. Holt Foundation; Join Hands, the Health and Safety Educational Alliance; the Microscopy Society of America (MSA); the Shell Oil Company Foundation; and the Crail-Johnson Foundation. GEMS gratefully acknowledges the contribution of word processing equipment from Apple Computer, Inc. This support does not imply responsibility for statements or views expressed in publications of the GEMS program.

Development and publication of this handbook has been supported in part by a grant from the National Science Foundation. In addition to NSF, the PEACHES program has been supported by grants from the Fund for the Improvement of Post-Secondary Education (FIPSE) and the Hewlett Packard Company.

For information on GEMS leadership and professional development opportunities, to receive a free catalog, the *GEMS Network News*, and PEACHES information, or if you have any comments, criticism, and suggestions—all are welcomed—please write or call:

University of California, Berkeley
GEMS
Lawrence Hall of Science # 5200
Berkeley, CA 94720-5200

(510) 642-7771

fax: (510) 643-0309

email: gems@uclink4.berkeley.edu

Web: www.lhs.berkeley.edu/GEMS

www.lhs.berkeley.edu/PEACHES

Acknowledgments

Development and publication of this handbook has been supported in part by a grant from the National Science Foundation (NSF) as part of the "Bridging Preschool and Kindergarten through Teacher Enhancement in Science and Mathematics" grant (ESI-9353447). Previous support for PEACHES came from the NSF "Enhancing Science Education for Preschool Educators" grant (TPE # 8954657). In addition to NSF, the PEACHES program has been supported by grants from the Fund for the Improvement of Post-Secondary Education (FIPSE) and the Hewlett Packard Company. The support of these organizations made PEACHES possible and extended our work as part of an active growing national network of early childcare educators.

The PEACHES participants who contributed to the early development of this handbook are listed after these introductory acknowledgments. Quotations from many of them are interspersed throughout the handbook. We greatly appreciate their suggestions and ideas.

This handbook is based on earlier versions, especially "Preschool Science and Math Explorations: The PEACHES Handbook for Educators" which was produced in December 1991 for participants in PEACHES workshops, courses, institutes, and related programs. Authors of that version include all of this handbook's authors.

The numerous teachers, preschool and daycare providers, early childhood specialists, and parents who assisted in testing units for the PEACHES and GEMS programs are listed at the front of each of the individual teacher guides. Their collective contribution has been immense, and we are very grateful to each and every one of them who helped make PEACHES and GEMS effective teacher- and parent-friendly materials. In addition, the following institutions and organizations collaborated with PEACHES to bring the program and materials to new audiences of preschool educators: the **BANANAS Child Care Information & Referral Center**, the **La Raza Information Center, Inc.**, **Los Medanos College, Merritt College, Pacific Oaks College Extension,** and **Northern Pacific Education.**

The authors extend a special thanks to the following educators who over the years supported the development of the PEACHES program, and who shared their wisdom and insights into the world of science and mathematics for young children.

Arlyce Currie
Marian C. Diamond
Karen Fong
Kathy Hagerty
Mimi Halferty
Rosario Herrera
Karen Lind
Lawrence Lowery
Myra Luciano
Karen Ostlund
Linda Rogers
Barbara Scales
Patsy Sherman
Susan Snyder
Elizabeth K. Stage
Steve Stripp
Jennifer Meux White

PEACHES 1990 and 1991 Course Participants

CALIFORNIA

Kimberly Agge
Mike Alcatraz
Pierrette Allison
Charlie M. Allums
Sylvia Alvarez-Mazzi
Terry Amgott-Kwan
Alma Arias
Kate Ashbey
Susie Ashley
Teresa Avila
Beverly Barrow
Betty Beasley
Cheryl Birden
Speranza Blackard
Ellastine Blalock
Debra Booze
Theresa Borges
Jonetta Bradford
Penelope Brody
Eufemia Buena Byrd
Trinidad Caselis
Willy Chen
Lucy Coleman
Yolanda Coleman-Wilson
Mary Conroy
Debbie Coyle
Idalina Cruz
Brooke H. B. D'Arezzo
Anastasia Decaristos
Evelynn DeLanis
Jeanne Devin
Lisa Dobbs
Marilyn C. Couglas
Arleen Dumin
Kawser Elshinawy
Margaret Engel
Sharon Espinoza
Iris Ezeb

> Since I've learned about PEACHES I find myself doing things differently. I was in a friend's front yard and she had some trees. I found myself looking on the branches and leaves for things I could find. Before this class I would have never done that! PEACHES has opened up my eyes to a new world. I look at science and my environment differently. I enjoy and feel comfortable teaching science. I think PEACHES is an excellent program for children. I feel if PEACHES has had an impact on how I now see things, imagine what it does for a child!"
>
> — *Robin Goodson*

Karen Fong
Elizabeth Fulton
Susan Galindo
Michelle Garabedian
Debbie Garcia
Karen A. Ghannadan
Robin Goodson
Deborah Green
Iris Greenbaum
Virginia Guadarrama
Mara Ellen Guckian
Elaine Guttman
Irma Guzman
Kathy Hagerty
Sallie Hanna-Rhyne
Matthew Heish
Judy Henry
Denise Hingle
Ortencia Hoopii
Patricia House
Bernice Huisman-Humbert
Patricia Hunter
Lucy Inouye
Barbara Jean Jackson
Tracy Johansing-Spittler
Maria A. Johnson-Price
Charlotte Johnson

Reather Jones
Stephanie Josey
Wendy Justice
Vanna Maria Kalofonos
Sharon Keane
Tara Kelly
Dena Keown
Margie M. Kirk
Nichelle R. Kitt
Marilyn Klemm
Nancy Kliszewski
Michele M. Knapp
Stella Ko Kwok
Sheryl Lambert
Paula Lawrence
Eileen Lok
Gayla Lucero
Filomena Macedo
Adwoa Mante
Pilar Marroquin
Juanita McAfee
Mary McCon
Mary T. McCormick
Silvia Mendez
Pamela Meredith
Richard Mermis
Franny Minervini-Zick

Denise Moyes-Schnur
Anasylvia Navarro
Rita Neely
Marcia Nybakken
Len Paterson
Lisa Payne
Grace Perry
Rosemarie Peterson
Katryna Prophet
Mary Raabe
Satinder Jit K. Rana
Denise M. Ratto
Kartyna Ray
Martha Ann Reed
Poppy Richie
Linda Rogers
Alice J. Romero
Cecilia Saffarian
Lee Ann Sanders
Terry Saugstad
Adrienne J. Schneider
Jenny Schwartz-Groody
Virginia Shelton
Patsy Sherman
Barbara Skaggs
Erin Smith
Uma Srinath

Adrienne Stitt
Vickie Stoller
Jonni Tannenbaum
Ella Tassin
Toni Teixeira

Ilda Terrazas
Barbara Terrell
Janice Thomas
Laura Todd
Tyra Toney

Oletha R. Wade
Diane Wallace
Inez Watson
Celestine Whittaker
Kim Wilcox

Rosalia Wilkins
Pam Wofford
Doris Wührmann
Caroline W. Yee

PEACHES 1994 Summer Institute Participants

CALIFORNIA
Farida Abawi
Lisa Arndt
Arella Barlev
Alice Bristol
Ernestine Brooks
Kelly Bye
Nicki Centeno
Sheryl Chan
Debra Cuevas
Evelynn Delanis
Mary Ehler
Nadine Farris
Maria Glidewell
Iris Greenbaum
Tiffany Harrison

Doris Henschel
Rosario Herrera
Myrna Lapres
Gladys Miller
Serra Mok
José Nuñez
Mina Radjabi
Linda Rayford

Poppy Richie
Lucille Rivera
Beverly Robinson
Jeniene Rodrigues
Jill Roy
Kouei Seng Saechao
Angela Samsel
Ann Steinbronn

Liz Sullivan
Louise Taub
Sarah Traderman
Tuyet Anh Tran
Joan Tryfter
Aileen Venable
Lupe Vigil
Debra Ziegler

> P reparing the unit was just as fun as presenting the unit. The information and directions of the booklet were clear and easy to follow. The posters and templates are wonderful. I didn't know how easy it could be to present math concepts with science to preschoolers and have a great time!"
> — *Karen Fong*

PEACHES 1995 Summer Institute Participants

ARIZONA
Hope Dillon
Pamela J. Garvin
Luci Gonzalez
Karla Heleotes
Lana Horn

CALIFORNIA
Rita Bailey
Deborah Barnett
Janet Bremond-Jones
Linda Campopiano

Maggie Chaffee
Amapola Franzen
Carmen Guerrero
Kathlyn Langs
Ellen Nishioka
Huong Thu Nguyen
Carol Parsons
Linda Petrich
Antoinette Phillips
Mary Queen
Theresa Reed
Tracy Saechao

Christina Torres
Margie Van Winkle
Melinda Will
Patricia Williams
Carol Wright

COLORADO
Domitilia Ortiz-Valdez
Melanie Poulson
Kathy Ocheltree
Sal Turner
Yvonne Tafoya

UTAH
Eileen Bernards
Louann Brough
Sunee Folkman
Judy Jackson
Sally R. Ogilvie

WASHINGTON
Marcia Boyd
Lucia Diaz
Ann Kumata
Liana Mix Nakamura
Jenny Parker
Sharon Travers

PEACHES 1996 Summer Institute Participants

CALIFORNIA
Jody Anderson
Kimberly Barry
Angela Cambell
Annette Henderson
Leah Marks
Magdalena Mejia
Mary Neumann
Julie Valdivia

FLORIDA
Christopher Dugan
Diane Egan
Carol Marino
Joyce Parent
Peggy Stokes

INDIANA
Rebecca Barloga
Judy Lazar
Maria Magaña
Milagros Vazquez
Maxine Wash

MINNESOTA
Sandy Asleson
Belinda Freeman
Michael Paul Gallo
Marilyn Labrensz
Bobbe Shreve

NEW YORK
Jeanine Dowd
Gail Feeley
Lisa Murray
Arlene Ransom
Christine Tibbetts

OHIO
Anne Dorsey
Marie George
Karen Kresser
Sally Moomaw
Terry Robertson

SOUTH CAROLINA
Kay Bartz
Lorraine Conrad
Melissa Klosterman
Kathryn Parrish
Felecia Philson

TEXAS (Austin)
Tina Otto
Holly Trantham
Deborah Buehler

(Houston)
Myra Luciano
Phyllis Berman
Cathy Homer

Table of Contents

What Is LHS?

LHS ★ *Lawrence Hall of Science • University of California at Berkeley*

The Lawrence Hall of Science (LHS) is a public science center on the University of California at Berkeley campus. LHS offers a full program of activities for the public. LHS is also a center for teacher education and curriculum research and development. Both the Great Explorations in Math and Science (GEMS) and the Primary Explorations for Children and Educators in Science (PEACHES) programs are integral parts of the Lawrence Hall of Science. Many GEMS and PEACHES curriculum units evolved from activities originated and taught by LHS educators over many years.

When the Lawrence Hall of Science was established more than 30 years ago, it was in response to a growing interest in hands-on science and mathematics education. It was natural that one of the Hall's main audiences would be young children. After all, children "do science" from the time they are born—they are curious about the world around them and actively explore the immediate environment using their senses. They learn to do new things, trying again if it doesn't seem to work, practicing things over and over, and enjoying their success when they gain a new ability or understanding. They ask questions and share their ideas with others. Children are natural scientists!

Early on, LHS began to offer workshops for children ages 2–3 and their parents, after school classes for 3– to 7-year-olds, and weekly visits for preschool and primary school classes. These classes and programs continue today. In fact, a number of preschools bring their groups to LHS classes regularly, just as they have for the past 20 years! These classes, such as "Getting To Know Animals," "Making Mud Pies with Mom and Dad," and "Storybook Math," all involve lots of doing, playing, exploring, thinking, and sharing. Children investigate live animals, build symmetrical structures with geometric shapes, or work with collections of buttons to discover, describe, and classify their attributes. What all LHS classes share is evident from the enthusiastic feedback from parents and teachers—children thrive on **active learning**. If the discoveries are engaging and meaningful, children are motivated to keep learning and share it with others. Many years of devising and refining a wide range of activities, extensive teacher and parent feedback, and formal evaluation studies all show that educational experiences like these spark tremendous excitement for discovering, exploring, and inquiring. In developing, designing, and refining GEMS and PEACHES activities, we take into account the many exciting new discoveries about how we learn, and innovative approaches in modern educational theory.

Our efforts at LHS are entirely consistent with the goals spelled out in *Science for All Americans*. This document, developed in 1989 by the American Association for the Advancement of Science (AAAS) Project 2061, outlined what today's educators need to do to advance scientific literacy and to prepare people—all people—to use scientific ways of thinking to make informed decisions, think critically, and solve real-world problems: "Today's young people will, as adults, greatly influence what life on earth will be like in 2061, the year Halley's Comet next returns. Being literate in science is a condition for [influencing life on earth] responsibly, as well as for living a full and interesting life."

What Is GEMS?

 **LHS GEMS** *Great Explorations in Math and Science*

S tudents sort and classify buttons or leaves, waddle around like penguins on ice, explore a strange green substance said to come from a distant planet, play a math game from China or Africa, or solve a "crime" with chemistry—all this is GEMS. Students learn best by doing—the basis of the GEMS approach. It is an approach backed by overwhelming educational evidence. Activities first engage students in direct experience and experimentation, before introducing explanations of principles and concepts. Utilizing easily obtained and inexpensive materials, GEMS activities allow teachers without special background in science or mathematics to successfully present hands-on, minds-on experiences.

Developed at the University of California at Berkeley's Lawrence Hall of Science, and tested in thousands of classrooms nationwide, more than 55 GEMS teacher's guides offer a wide spectrum of learning opportunities from preschool through 10th grade.

Emphasis on teamwork and cooperative learning, the use of a wide variety of learning formats, and reliance on direct experience rather than textbooks makes GEMS highly appropriate for use with populations that have been historically underrepresented in science and mathematics careers. In GEMS activities, students are encouraged to work together to discover more, explore a problem, or solve a mystery, rather than fixating on the so-called right answer, or engaging in negatively competitive behavior. Cooperative (or collaborative) learning is one of the most effective strategies for bridging and appreciating differences and diversities of background and culture. It is also one of the most effective ways to prepare students for the workplaces of the future.

The GEMS series interweaves a number of educational ideas and goals. GEMS units strongly support the inquiry-driven, activity-based approach to science and mathematics education, and spell out how that approach can be practically presented, by veteran and inexperienced teachers, to the enormous benefit of all students. GEMS guides encompass important learning objectives, summarized on the front page of each guide under the headings of *Skills, Concepts, Themes, Mathematics Strands,* and *Nature of Science and Mathematics.* These objectives can be directly and flexibly related to national standards and benchmarks, other science and mathematics curricula, state frameworks, and district guidelines.

Since classroom testing began in 1984, more than 600,000 teachers and at least eight million students have taken part in GEMS activities. In collaboration with thousands of teachers, GEMS activities are adapted for the classroom, and for teachers who may not have special background in math and science. A rapidly expanding national network of teachers and educators take part in GEMS Leader's and Associate's workshops and receive a free national newsletter, the *GEMS Network News.* There are now more than 35 GEMS Centers or Network Sites nationwide, providing support to teachers through workshops and diverse professional development opportunities.

GEMS Activity Guides and Handbooks

GEMS teacher's guides contain instructions for presenting inquiry-based, guided-discovery science and mathematics activities in the classroom. In addition to teacher's guides, there are several guides written with other science centers or schoolwide discovery labs in mind; two assembly program presenter's guides, and two tabletop exhibit guides. While not originally intended for teachers, the exhibit and assembly guides can be adapted for effective use by teachers in the classroom. The annual GEMS catalog carries brief descriptions of all GEMS guides and handbooks. All GEMS activity guides are rich with ideas for presenting science and mathematics in meaningful, effective, and exciting ways.

As the number of GEMS activity guides increased, so did interest in using these guides in a variety of situations and from differing perspectives. The teacher's and leader's handbooks give practical suggestions for using GEMS in the context of a classroom, school, district, or statewide science program. The *GEMS Teacher's Handbook* is an introduction to the philosophy and approach of GEMS, with some suggested curriculum sequences. The *GEMS Leader's Handbook* is particularly useful for teachers and educators who have been trained as GEMS Leaders or GEMS Associates, or any teachers familiar with GEMS who want to introduce GEMS to others on a schoolwide or district level. It includes a series of articles on the educational effectiveness of the GEMS approach. Additional GEMS handbooks include discussions of key educational issues. *The Rainbow of Mathematics* shines its multicolored light on the "M" in GEMS. *Science and Math Explorations for Young Children* focuses on the crucial early learning years. *A Parent's Guide to Great Explorations in Math and Science* describes ways parents can use GEMS activities at home, as a basis for a science or math fair project, or as a way to volunteer in the community or classroom. *The Architecture of Reform* describes how GEMS relates to the science education reform movement and the *National Science Education Standards.* Another handbook, *Once Upon A GEMS Guide: Connecting Young People's Literature to Great Explorations in Math and Science,* annotates more than 400 literary selections that can be used beneficially with math and science activities. The *Insights & Outcomes* handbook details how to provide active assessment for GEMS activities and provides numerous assessment case studies with actual student work.

GEMS is a growing series. New guides and handbooks are being developed constantly and current guides are revised frequently. We welcome your comments, suggestions, and letters. Let us hear from you.

What Is PEACHES?  Primary Explorations for Children and Educators in Science

Imagine children closely observing a trail of ants outdoors, pretending to be scout ants in search of food, feeding ants in an ant farm, or playing a cooperative math game called "Fill the Hill." This is PEACHES! Young children learn best through activities that build concepts and skills in an integrated, hands-on, engaging way. Teachers find PEACHES activities easy to present, without requiring a special background in science or math for successful presentation. Science and math concepts and skills are interwoven with other key areas of an early childhood program to benefit the whole child.

In 1989, the PEACHES program was launched at the University of California's Lawrence Hall of Science through major grants from the Department of Education Fund for the Improvement of Post Secondary Education (FIPSE), the National Science Foundation (NSF) Teacher Enhancement program, and the Hewlett-Packard Company. These grants allowed us to work with preschool teachers, childcare centers, home daycare providers, after school program instructors, and kindergarten teachers in a formal and organized way.

PEACHES activities have been used in elementary schools, preschools, childcare centers, family day care sites, and homes. With modifications, the activities can be adapted for use with 3-year-olds and with children above first grade. Teacher's guides are designed so teachers, childcare providers, and parents can feel knowledgeable, confident, and above all, excited about doing science and math with their children.

PEACHES is now a nationally recognized early childhood program.

PEACHES has joined forces with the Great Explorations in Math and Science (GEMS) program to further trial-test and publish selected PEACHES units. As a result of their further development in GEMS, the PEACHES units are refined through a series of national field tests and published in step-by-step teacher's guide format with numerous illustrations and photographs, and with expanded special sections on assessment and literature.

In its professional development programs, through workshops, college courses, conferences, institutes and school inservice programs; PEACHES has reached more than 3,000 early childhood educators, parents, day care providers, and others who work with children ages 4–6.

GEMS guides drawn from PEACHES are among the most widely used and distributed. They are *Ladybugs, Tree Homes, Penguins and Their Young, Tree Homes, Eggs Eggs Everywhere, Ant Homes Under the Ground,* and *Mother Opossum and Her Babies.*

A number of other GEMS science and math guides also feature activities for the early childhood range: *Buzzing A Hive; Hide A Butterfly; Animal Defenses; Frog Math; Group Solutions; Group Solutions, Too!; Treasure Boxes; Liquid Explorations; Involving Dissolving; Sifting Through Science;* and *Secret Formulas.* There are also several K–6 GEMS guides: *Terrarium Habitats; Bubble Festival; Build It! Festival;* and *Investigating Artifacts.*

Together this collection adds up to a rich resource for early childhood educators. These units are effective enrichment for many different core curricula. They can be linked to each other in a variety of ways to build deeper understanding, or can be used individually as stand-alone units to provide students with exciting and fulfilling early math and science experiences.

There are also a few PEACHES guides developed in the early 1990s still to be published through GEMS. We look forward to the new millennium and making these remaining guides—and new ones, too—part of the GEMS/PEACHES series and available to teachers and childcare providers nationwide.

Introduction

This handbook is meant to help you understand the educational philosophy and practice of the PEACHES and GEMS programs, and to assist you in using GEMS/PEACHES teacher's guides at your school or child center. It outlines techniques and strategies that we find successful with young students, and describes how the activities emphasize a developmental approach.

On a larger level, it is intended as a useful summary of current ideas in early childhood education that may help you evaluate all curriculum materials and spark your own ideas about new directions to take in your educational efforts.

Our goal is to help children build from what they already know in order to construct new knowledge and ideas. The PEACHES program has four main goals.

1. Increase teacher confidence and foster positive attitudes about teaching science and mathematics.

2. Expand teacher understanding of science and mathematics content.

3. Present appropriate science activities and discuss the relevant content and pedagogy supporting each lesson.

4. Develop and document the lessons and teaching strategies into teacher's guides for educators nationwide to use with their children.

At the back of this handbook are descriptions of the *National Science Education Standards* and National Council of Teachers of Mathematics (NCTM) *Principles and Standards for School Mathematics* along with all the GEMS and GEMS/PEACHES early childhood guides published so far that connect with those standards. A chart correlating the science and math standards with the GEMS/PEACHES and GEMS guides is also included for easy reference (pages 62–63).

Since this handbook focuses on early childhood, we selected five of the eight K–4 content standards from the *National Science Education Standards*. Some elements of all standards are more relevant to the upper end of the grade range (grades 3 and 4) and we provided short notes to highlight those aspects that relate best to early childhood (preschool through grade 2) in the descriptions of the individual standards. (The standards not detailed here are "Unifying Concepts and Processes," "Science and Technology," and "History and Nature of Science.")

We view the selected five standards as particularly relevant for the early childhood curriculum. A check mark (✓) indicates that a significant portion of the GEMS/PEACHES unit makes a meaningful connection to one or more of the major categories under that standard. This connection could be to the learning content of the unit as a whole, to several activities in it, or to only one activity, so long as it makes a strong connection. For example, in the last activity of *Eggs Eggs Everywhere* (which is mostly Life Science related), students explore the movements of plastic eggs and other objects on flat and inclined surfaces. This is the reason for the check mark under "Physical Science," relating to the Physical Science subcategory "Motions and Forces."

In regard to the mathematics standards for grades PreK–2, we selected six of the 10 standards from the *Principles and Standards for School Mathematics.* That document contains content standards as well as standards on instructional practices integral to implement all the standards. In the chart, we look at all five of the content standards and a key instructional standard—Problem Solving. The remaining four standards ("Reasoning and Proof," "Communication," "Representation," and "Connections") are discussed on page 42.

Overall, we support the crucial task of providing excellent math and science education for young children.

Chapter 1

Science for Everyone

We all experience science every day! Science can mean noticing the rainbows in rain puddles and rain clouds, or finding out what's in your backyard. Science is following the growth of a young child or making a new recipe. Our environment provides a wealth of interesting things to wonder about and explore. To paraphrase Ralph Waldo Emerson, "People love to wonder, and that is the seed of science."

Learning science in our daily surroundings can be as exciting for adults as it is for children. While you and your children are following an ant trail, you are sharing observations, making comparisons, and asking questions. The methods you use in your investigations are as important as the facts you learn. Science is about both **how** and **what** you learn. As teachers and parents of young children, you have the pleasure of sharing this process of discovery with youngsters who have an unlimited curiosity about the world around them.

Learning Science

Science challenges people to go beyond the knowledge others have discovered. For this reason, science is much more than a collection of facts—it is a process for exploring the universe. Science provides a way to inquire about the world and an opportunity to learn new things about our environment.

Scientists use many skills to conduct their research activities. These same skills are basic to all human learning. A growing child develops the skills that will help her explore her world. These skills continue to be used throughout life.

- **OBSERVING** and using all the senses.

- **COMPARING** things and events by looking for similarities and differences in such properties as color, shape, length, number, and action.

- **FINDING RELATIONSHIPS** and integrating new information and events with past experiences.

- **ORGANIZING** and grouping things and information.

- **COMMUNICATING** and sharing information with others by touching, telling, drawing, making things, playing, enacting ideas, recording, asking questions, and writing information.

- **EXPERIMENTING** and manipulating things and situations in a systematic way, playing, and exploring.

- **INFERRING** by looking for cause-and-effect relationships based on observation.

- **PREDICTING** by making educated guesses about the outcome of events.

- **APPLYING** information and skills to new situations.

- **SOLVING** dilemmas and problems using a combination of all these skills.

The inquiry approach to learning science makes science dynamic and relevant for people of all ages, and helps them develop the thinking skills needed in today's technological society.

Developmentally Appropriate Practice

The past 15 years have seen a dramatic increase in the need for high quality, early childhood education. Not only are many more children attending child care and preschool programs, research shows that early experiences are crucial to future success in school and throughout life. Research also emphasizes the need to address children's developmental levels when designing learning environments and curriculum.

Because of this pressing need to outline the best practices for early childhood educators, the National Association for the Education of Young Children (NAEYC) published *Developmentally*

Appropriate Practice in Early Childhood Programs —a handbook that describes 12 principles of development and learning for developmentally appropriate practice. The PEACHES and GEMS programs strongly support all of these principles, particularly the following.

> *Areas of children's development—physical, social, emotional, and cognitive—are closely related. Development in one area influences and is influenced by development in other areas.*

Our activities emphasize important science and mathematics concepts by embedding them in experiences that promote social interactions, personal reflection, and physical development. Children are involved in dramatic play where they pretend to be opossums or ladybugs defending themselves from predators. Ice and water activities encourage children to work together to discover how colors blend and ice melts. All activities build language and communication skills as learners discuss their observations and findings with each other and with adults.

> *Children are active learners, drawing on direct physical and social experience as well as culturally transmitted knowledge to construct their own understandings of the world around them.*

Each lesson supports active thinkers and "do-ers" as children observe earthworm behavior, sort toy bears by size, or enact the ladybug life cycle from egg to adult. Topics and themes are built around what children are familiar with and what interests and motivates them to discover more. The process of active learning in turn prepares students to go further and investigate new questions and topics that arise.

> *Play is an important vehicle for children's social, emotional, and cognitive development, as well as a reflection of their development.*

Free play and dramatic play are important elements of GEMS/PEACHES activities. Allowing children to manipulate materials freely without structure helps them learn at their own level and rate. Dramatic play encourages the "acting out" of abstract concepts, such as life cycles and defensive behaviors, making the ideas concrete and real. Teachers find play an excellent opportunity to assess what children know and want to learn.

> *Development advances when children have opportunities to practice newly acquired skills as well as when they experience a challenge just beyond the level of their present mastery.*

Activities build on what children have learned before and encourage them to apply new skills to new situations. These challenges are often in the form of investigations, such as exploring ice melting or estimating the number of pockets their classmates are wearing. Children are pushed to extend their learning and mastery of new skills in fun and exciting contexts.

> *Children demonstrate different modes of knowing and learning and different ways of representing what they know.*

PEACHES and GEMS lessons are presented in various ways to acknowledge the differences in learning modes. Hands-on investigation with real animals or objects, storytelling and dramatic play, creating models, taking part in simulations, and playing games all lend themselves to stimulating learning in ways that respond to the different strengths and abilities of each child. The multiplicity and ongoing nature of these approaches also allows for authentic assessment of student knowledge and skills as an integral part of the curriculum.

Overall, GEMS/PEACHES activities select key content and skills in science and mathematics and present it in a way that addresses children's past experiences, culture, interests, and developmental levels. Teachers find the lessons to be effective in teaching math and science concepts in an integrated way, emphasizing language development as well as development of the whole child.

Chapter 2 Science and Math Explorations with Children

People often ask preschool teachers, "What do you teach in preschool besides how to play with other children?" Teachers answer, "Plenty!" In a typical preschool classroom, the children's enthusiasm for learning through playful exploration is readily apparent. Activities that involve the senses, exploration, creative play, and verbalization are basic to the young child's construction of knowledge.

The discovery approach to teaching and learning presents science in a non-threatening way. Through hands-on, minds-on experiences, factual information and new ideas are acquired. Just as importantly, young students develop skills to investigate any new substance, object, or event in the world around them. As they investigate, they begin to build a foundation of basic concepts that will start them on the road to scientific and mathematical literacy.

Enjoying what you do builds learning and confidence. Built into the units are activities that develop self-esteem, confidence, cooperation, and problem-solving skills. Children come away from the activities feeling successful. Their increased feeling of competence carries over to everyday activities at school and home.

A child was added to my class from a younger age group. He was not ready for the change; he was upset, felt out of place, and stood to the side of the class dejectedly. I was doing a ladybug role-play with my children thinking this child was not even listening. At the end of class we went outdoors. He went to some of the friends he had from the previous class and did the complete role-play in exact sequence and was having a wonderful time—his dejectedness forgotten."

— *Sharon Espinoza*

Exploring with the Senses

Inquiry-based activities foster children's excitement about exploring the world with their senses. Children observe ladybugs, compare their hands to an opossum paw print, crawl through a classroom "ant tunnel," and eat a popsicle "aphid."

In *Penguins and Their Young*, children pretend to be penguins snuggling together to keep warm. Huddled side by side, each child feels the warmth of the group increasing as they press closer together. Through role-playing, the children compare this penguin-warming behavior to something they might do themselves on a cold winter day. This approach emphasizes experiences that are relevant in a young child's life.

The activities promote caring attitudes toward the environment, and feature animals and their homes that are familiar to young children. They may have seen them in storybooks, their backyards, or at the zoo. Many of the small animals may be observed and touched in a classroom terrarium. Along with the living world, activities examine the physical world of water, ice, sand, soil, as well as physical processes, such as rolling, sinking, and floating.

cience can be simple. After talking about trees and the fall using the cardboard tree [in Tree Homes], one boy in particular was amazed at the trees he saw as we walked to the park each day. It was as if he had never seen a tree before! He pointed them out to me and told me the color and shape of the leaves."

— Laura Todd

Recording Observations Through Projects

In many GEMS/PEACHES units, children put together paper models of animals by observing and matching the spatial relationships of real animal structures, such as legs, eyes, antennae, and wings. These projects provide youngsters who cannot write with a way to record their observations. The processes of comparing, orienting, and assembling objects are essential aspects of science and mathematics.

For example, in the PEACHES unit *Homes in a Pond* (not yet published as a GEMS guide), children begin by making an aquarium home for live fish and observe the fish swim, hide, and eat. In a companion activity, children make paper fish and pretend that their fish eat paper flies and plants, which then get glued inside the fish. Children "swim" their play fish to a blue paper pond where they act out fish behavior using props such as logs, plants, and toy snakes.

Although these lessons focus on the science-related topic of fish and ponds, the paper activity may not at first appear to reinforce any math or science skills. However, if you view the paper fish as a recording tool, the math and science processes become apparent. The children compare the paper fish to real fish. They use their understanding of symmetry, as they assemble their paper fish, to determine the position of eyes, mouth, fins, and stomach. In their play sessions, they count body parts and manipulate the fish as if it were real.

These teacher-directed recording sessions (the construction and manipulation of the paper fish) should not be confused with creative art and drama. They provide a way for children to exhibit and review what they have learned, and to use basic math and science skills to organize their observations. At home, these projects can be a source of continued play as the children re-enact stories for family members. We recommend that you follow the project and drama sessions in many GEMS/PEACHES units with creative art and play time for the children to pursue their own interests. Frequently their paintings and creations will lead to rich and unusual extensions of the activities.

Chapter 3 The Role of Teachers and Parents

The best way to learn science is to do it! Even with little or no background in science, you can learn how to teach science and discover the excitement of investigating the natural world. You are encouraged to learn right along with your children as they observe small garden animals, participate in dramas, make models, and experiment with household materials.

By providing a choice of materials and situations for youngsters, you and your children can guide this process of exploration. Take the time to let concepts and the wonders of nature evolve from the activities as you learn together. This learning will be connected to prior experiences of the children as they answer their own questions, solve their own problems, and generate their own ways of organizing their world.

Checklist for Supporting Science Exploration

Children blossom in a safe and fun setting that encourages them to investigate and communicate their observations. The following are some ways of building children's self-esteem while helping them become successful explorers.

- **BE SENSITIVE** and supportive of children's personalities, interests, learning styles, and backgrounds. Don't force children to participate—some may be observing and learning from a distance.

- **ENCOURAGE** children to observe and describe what is happening. This process is a very important part of language development.

- **OFFER** children different ways to communicate and record what they have learned, such as making models and puppets, telling stories, playing, enacting dramas.

- **HELP** children to investigate their own questions and state their questions in ways that can be investigated: "What do you think will happen if the ice cube is left on the table?" "Where do you think the pill bug will go in the garden?"

- **ENCOURAGE** children to make guesses and predictions.

- **FACILITATE** discussions to assist children in sharing ideas and experiences.

When we were given earthworms I was excited. I brought them back to my school where the other teachers were not as excited. In my class I set out the two worms on some dirt. We named them Charlie. The kids were excited to watch them and touch them. The next day a boy brought in more worms and other kids asked their teachers if they could have Charlies too! The kids drew the teachers in and soon every room had Charlies!"

— *Lucy Coleman*

As I was teaching the ladybug unit I would bring the aquariums—teeming with lady bugs—home on the weekends so they could be fed aphids. The ladybugs had a prominent place on my kitchen counter and I couldn't stop watching them. I saw them eat, mate, lay eggs, fight, and die. One late night my husband 'caught me' leaning on the counter and staring at my little friends. He had a brief remark, 'You're obsessed!' He was right, I was!"

— *Lee Ann Sanders*

Developing a Science and Math Program for Your Classroom

As a teacher of young children, you know the importance of creating learning environments that fit the needs of each individual child. This can be a difficult task, especially when you have a group of students with differing developmental needs and interests. Math and science can help address your children's diverse needs by providing hands-on, minds-on activities that build content and skills, not only in math and science, but in other areas as well—such as language, fine and large motor skills, and social skill development. Science and math can also provide opportunities to assess student learning in ways that mirror the diverse ways that children learn. Keep the following guidelines in mind when selecting activities and materials for your program.

- **WELCOME** and **BUILD UPON** children's ideas and input, even if the ideas don't seem to relate to the activity. If children provide incorrect information, help them make more observations when possible. Continue to guide them toward discovering more accurate information. Sometimes, you may also need to tell them what others have discovered.

- **ARRANGE** opportunities for children to teach others and share their experiences in their own words. This often happens naturally through play.

- **PROVIDE** materials and space for free exploration, and encourage children to pursue their own creative interests.

- **PLAN** materials and space for each activity and be flexible enough to allow children to pursue new directions their activities may take.

- **CHOOSE** only a few activities to present at one time and take your time in order to do them well with the children. Less can be more!

- **AVOID** passing along your own fears to your children.

- **INVITE** parent involvement and help parents extend the activities at home.

- Children need to be involved in **active investigations** with **concrete materials.** These investigations should encourage inquiry and problem-solving skills, including observing, comparing, sharing ideas, asking questions, and recording. Children should do activities that engage them physically and mentally while investigating materials they can manipulate and use in ways they discover and initiate. Look for ways to **sequence and extend** single activities to develop a full program of **articulated learning opportunities.**

- Activities should be **interesting** and **engaging** to young children, **relevant** to their lives and the world around them. Look for activities that spark a child's interest and that have meaning to their lives in and outside of class. Connections to topics common to all cultures and daily life can be more meaningful than catering to what is currently commercially popular and promoted through the media.

- Incorporate **play** in all its forms, including **dramatic, creative, games,** and **free play.** Play is not only active but is an opportunity for young children to "work-out" or construct new learning. Play builds an important foundation for later abstract thinking and greatly contributes to language and social development. Concepts and skills in math and science can be expressed and reinforced through play.

- Use **children's literature** and **storytelling** to set interesting contexts for the science and math concepts you are studying. This provides an opportunity to develop language and thinking skills while supporting math/science content learning in an engaging way.

- Promote **writing**, including dictation and invented writing, as well as **drawing,** as opportunities to share, compare, record, and communicate what your children learn and want to learn.

- **Integrate lessons** with math and different areas of science (life, earth, physical) to provide a rich content and to emphasize the important "connections" among these areas. Nature and life science topics provide a good hook for young children (and teachers too!) while giving plenty of opportunities to weave in math, physical science, and earth science.

- Emphasize **respect** and **appreciation** of the **living** and **physical world.** Love of nature can build a growing social and environmental awareness. This kind of learning can be fun and enjoyable while building self-confidence and positive attitudes toward math and science.

- Include **opportunities for parents and families** to participate in the activities. This can happen in the classroom or at home where children can readily share their projects or conduct similar investigations with family members.

- Include **flexible** lessons that allow you to **adapt** and **modify** them to your own program, needs, and interests of your children. Look for ways to **extend activities** and to use existing activities from your program to build on and further student learning.

- Overall, lessons need to be **developmentally appropriate.** They should be based on what educators and you know about how children learn and develop within the cognitive, social, emotional, and physical domains of development. Math and science can assist you in providing a program that helps children develop skills in all of these domains, while fostering abilities and conveying content that will enable them to think mathematically and scientifically in our rapidly changing world.

Parents Make the Difference

Even with little or no background in science and math, if you as parents have enthusiasm for learning and a child as your companion, you can make many delightful and important discoveries together!

The enthusiasm you demonstrate for your child's school activities and home projects sends the message that learning is important and fun. Your support and involvement at home through reading, conversation, exploration, and play provides an important foundation for your child's continuing success in school. Talk with your child's teacher about your interest in assisting with an activity in the classroom, and plan a time that fits into your schedule.

When your child begins preschool, so begins a new chapter in your own discovery process as a teacher within the home.

Become an observer of learning as you encourage your child to share the materials and activities he brings home. Provide a display area where pictures and projects become prompts for further conversation and activities. Invite your child to teach you new things he has learned to give him experience applying new skills and ideas. Together select items to put into a portfolio, and each week enjoy a quiet time together looking over his growing collection of accomplishments.

Youngsters explore the natural world with a passion and curiosity that is awesome to adults. Encourage your child to be your guide and the instigator of investigations in the garden, the kitchen, and the bathtub. Open-ended questions such as "What do you see, hear, smell, feel, taste?" stimulate observations, predictions, and further investigation. As the two of you talk about your adventures and plans, your child is building language and thinking skills.

Clean-up time provides an opportunity for children to develop organizational skills. A disorderly pile of materials can become the site of a sorting game. Save some time at the end of activities to model and participate in a playful re-organization process. Household routines such as matching socks and sorting containers for recycling can be fun ways for youngsters to demonstrate their skills. Challenges such as "How many crayons can you put in the box?" "Can you sort these into big blocks and little blocks?" "What do you think is the best way to wipe all these crumbs into the basket?" "Can we clean this up before the big hand on the clock points to 3?" are useful strategies for promoting cooperation and spatial learning.

The following anecdote illustrates how one parent avoided letting her fears of small garden animals interfere with her daughter's fascination with snails.

I had a parent who drove all the way back from work to drop off the snails her daughter had collected and forgotten to take to school. The mother knew how disappointed her daughter would be if she didn't have the snails. Even though the mother was afraid of the snails and didn't want to touch them, she came walking in with the bag of snails held at arm's length!"

— *Sharon Espinoza*

Decades of research studies point to parent involvement in a child's education as the single most important factor for academic success—more important than a parent's own situation, background, or education.

Research on student performance identifies parent support at home and parent participation in educational activities at school as key predictors of student success. Many parents may not be aware of this research, or know what is meant by "parent involvement," or have a clear idea of how they go about playing the role of an involved parent. This could be called one of the "best-kept secrets" in educational research—it needs to be known and understood much more widely.

The encouraging news is that "being involved" doesn't require knowledge of math or science, a college education, or any extensive preparation. There are a collection of concrete actions, many of them small, that together can make a huge difference for children. The GEMS program is developing new parent education program materials, titled "Preparing Active Partners in Education: Tools for the Education of Parents and Other Caregivers" that your school or center may be interested in obtaining to help your own parent education and involvement programs.

Not only has research clearly established the rewards to individual students of having their parents more involved with their education and schooling, **there is strong evidence that parent involvement is one of the key factors that determines if a school is an "effective" school. Studies show parent involvement greatly improves the overall quality of schools.**

Schools that find ways to work well with families have higher student achievement, improved teacher morale, higher ratings of teachers by parents, more support from families, and better reputations in the community. This has been shown to be the case in both low- and high-resource communities. Reaching out to the broadest cross-section of parents is key to ensuring the greatest benefits for your school community and all students.

Chapter 4 Children's Play and Creativity

One of the universal characteristics of children is their capacity to play. Play is an essential feature of any early childhood program. Play contributes to a child's social, emotional, and cognitive growth. And, equally important, playing is just plain fun! Play can take many forms, however, it is always freely chosen and directed by the child.

In any PEACHES guide, there is a mix of teacher-directed and child-directed activities. Although more time is spent describing teacher-directed activities, the PEACHES philosophy promotes equal time for children to pursue spontaneous and creative play. By its very nature, play is free from instruction on the part of adults. In a play area, adults should serve as facilitators for the safe use of materials and spaces.

Where Does Play Fit into PEACHES?

In the guides there are suggestions for linking specific science and math content to children's play. For example, in *Eggs Eggs Everywhere*, a basket of colorful plastic eggs is made available for children to play with in whatever way they choose. They may use them in the housekeeping corner pretending to cook breakfast; they may practice opening and closing them and mixing two differently colored halves; they may fill them with sand or water. Whether exploring the physical properties of the eggs or incorporating them into dramatic play, each child can pursue her own ideas by selecting an activity that suits her interests. Later, when the children sort the eggs by color in a structured group activity, their previous experience of playing with the eggs will make it easier for them to concentrate on the single characteristic of color.

In the activity (from the same guide) "Animals That Hatch From Eggs," the children are again given the opportunity to play freely with the eggs. This time the children discover tiny toy animals inside the eggs. In this way, they learn about animals that hatch from eggs in a fun and self-motivated fashion. The eggs and animals can be used by the children at the playdough table, the block corner, or wherever else the children's imaginations take them.

My children have been using the playground for a new kind of dramatic play that the PEACHES units inspired. The slide becomes an iceberg and mommy and daddy penguins plunged down the iceberg into the sea. A leopard seal (which is usually me) chases them back to the "iceberg ladder." The climbing structure is also a tree home for raccoons, and owls, and their families."

— *Poppie Richie*

My 3-year-olds were enthralled with ladybugs and ladybug food. For over one week, the children paired off in the yard wearing their wings and pretending to "eat" the aphids off our small fruit trees."

— *Terry Amgott-Kwan*

Play is an important time for children to process new concepts and information. Children initiate their own ways of reviewing and reinforcing what has been presented to them in PEACHES activities. Teachers who used the curriculum in their program tell us the children's daily play often incorporates ideas from PEACHES activities.

The paper models constructed by the children become props for dramatic play. For example, in *Penguins and Their Young*, paper-bag penguins swim in the "ocean" and slide on the "ice." In *Mother Opossum and Her Babies*, children climb their paper baby opossums into trees and give them rides on their back. As students engage in this kind of pretend play, they incorporate the factual information they learn into imaginative scenarios.

The social interaction, language development, and creative expression inherent in play are valid reasons for letting children use materials in ways that are most meaningful to them.

Guidelines for Supporting Play

- Provide plenty of space and materials for children to try out their ideas. Leave toy animals and other props used in the dramas in play areas for children to use. Be sure to have extra props available so there are enough materials to be easily shared. Allow time for them to play with their animal projects before they take them home. For example, suggest they play with their clay turtles in the sandbox, or use building block tunnels for their paper ants.

- Carefully watch and learn from children's play about their interests, personalities, and developmental levels. Play reflects children's real-life experiences and understanding of the world. Observing your children at play is a wonderful opportunity to notice the themes important to children.

Notice who plays with whom and the roles each child takes in directing the play. How well do they cooperate? How do they resolve conflicts? When children incorporate subjects from activities into their play, use the opportunity to get feedback about what new concepts and vocabulary they learned.

- When necessary, guide and redirect children's play so it is productive. There may be times when you need to assist children if their play gets off track. If the play becomes unsafe, overly aggressive, or unfair to one of the players, you need to intercede. Otherwise, be supportive from the sidelines; let the children be in control of their play.

Using Science to Spark Children's Creativity

We often marvel at the elaborate, fanciful stories and art created by young children. Science and math activities can provide a rich source of character, setting, and materials for children to use in their creations. These inventions, whether they are sand projects or free-flowing plays, re-

veal how youngsters have integrated knowledge and skills and are using them in new situations.

Encourage and support the children's creative expression, even if it means delaying another scheduled activity. When you listen to children tell about their paintings, sculptures, and play sessions, you are encouraging their use of new words and ideas. At the same time you are given a window into their thought processes and an opportunity to assess their learning.

Young children are spontaneously creative so we need to be sensitive and flexible to enable them to pursue their ideas. Schedule time for child-directed activities to flow out of the organized science and math activities. The following is a checklist of teaching strategies that can improve your children's opportunities to be creative and to integrate science and mathematics with language and art.

- **Provide interesting free-play materials,** some of which relate to previous activities. Include a variety of materials such as paper and paints, materials for sculpture, props, and costumes.

- **Identify spaces or activity stations,** distinct from the hubbub of general activity, where the children can go to create things.

- **Respect ongoing activity** and whenever possible allow children to complete a project or scenario.

- **Observe these creative ventures.** Be aware of how children are applying what they learn and help them sustain their ideas.

- **Elicit the nature of the child's creative product** rather than giving it an adult interpretation. Try, "What have you made?" rather than, "Oh, what a lovely pond." Avoid directing or correcting a work in progress.

- **Acknowledge each child's creative efforts** in a way that encourages the child to talk about his or her product. "Tell me about your picture?"

At the end of the elephant unit my kindergarten class dictated elephant stories. I was amazed at how much they learned. Children with very little language and even limited-English speaking children developed factual vocabulary about elephants. One boy, who is very young developmentally and hardly ever on task, loved the dramatic play activities and was able to dictate this story: 'An elephant goes in the water. His feet walk in the water. A baby elephant go in the water. His floppy ears big.'"

— *Linda Rogers*

- **Write down, tape, or videotape** children's stories and plays so they can enjoy them again and experience a sense of accomplishment.

- **Educate parents about the value of creative expression in boys and girls.** Encourage parents to observe and document the creative process at home.

- **Observe children's creative efforts** as a way to evaluate how they extend and apply what they learn.

- **Plan and allow time for individual creative projects** as well as group projects.

PEACHES and an "Emergent Curriculum"

PEACHES worked closely with Hearts Leap School (a private preschool and kindergarten in Berkeley, California) in 1998 to learn how PEACHES activities could be used in a program that embraces an "emergent curriculum" approach.

In an emergent curriculum, planning emerges from the daily life of the children and adults in the program. Teachers build the curriculum around the interests, ideas, and experiences of their students. Teachers do not plan out the year, or even the next month, in advance. Rather, curriculum planning is a very open-ended process that unfolds to reflect the uniqueness of the children and teachers in a particular group.

How might PEACHES activities be implemented into that type of program?

To answer that question, PEACHES enlisted the help of Hearts Leap Director Judy Jones and teachers Vickie Stoller and Lois Cottrell. They attended numerous PEACHES teacher's workshops and acquired all the guides. Through many conversations and classroom observations with these talented educators, we discovered there was great overlap in our approaches to teaching science and math to young children. The GEMS/PEACHES curriculum and Hearts Leap's program had the following components in common.

- Topics selected are relevant to children's lives.
- Curriculum integrates science, math, drama, language, art, and movement.
- Investigations are hands-on and in-depth.
- The importance of play is emphasized.
- Opportunities for language development are valued and promoted.
- Ideas and concepts are explored through many learning styles and modalities.

For Hearts Leap teachers, GEMS/PEACHES guides proved a valuable resource which they pull off the shelf at opportune times as their emergent curriculum unfolds. Some activities are presented as written in the guides, others are modified, and some may not be done at all. They learned effective strategies from the guides, which they use as models for other subjects.

For example, using drama to present factual information is a technique that can be used to introduce any topic. "What I love about the dramas is that we use real language," said Judy Jones. "Kids are very thirsty for that. It's very empowering. We take great ideas from the guides and go beyond, webbing into other areas of the curriculum and creating a curriculum that is custom-made for our students."

Chapter 5 Language Development

Young children learn language best in an environment that provides them with a variety of interesting, concrete materials with which to interact.

In GEMS/PEACHES activities, students investigate live animals such as ladybugs and ants. They explore nature and engage in sensory activities.

The excitement of these activities stimulates descriptive language and a lively exchange of ideas. By asking open-ended questions such as "What is your ladybug doing?" or "What do you think is happening to the bubbles?" teachers encourage children to verbalize their observations and thoughts.

By genuinely listening to what students say, a teacher can gain insight into students' current understandings and can adapt the curriculum to take into account student interests.

Students' vocabulary is bound to increase. New vocabulary is introduced in context and with visual cues such as posters and dramas so students can easily grasp the meaning. New words are used repeatedly, which is the key to making them stick. Children like to use scientific words, but teachers must be careful not to overwhelm them with too much new vocabulary at one time. Take into account the ages and developmental levels of your students in deciding how much vocabulary to introduce.

Language and Play

Everyone who works with young children knows they love to pretend. GEMS/PEACHES units build on this passion for make-believe play by integrating role-playing and dramatic play into the curriculum. For example, in *Tree Homes*, children become bear cubs and snuggle together in caves made out of tables covered with sheets. In *Ladybugs*, children wear paper wings and "fly" around the yard. The animal projects created by

the students serve as props in creative play. In *Mother Opossum and Her Babies*, children role-play being mother opossums and carry their paper baby opossums around in paper bag pouches and on their backs. Additional realistic props (toy animals, scenery, pretend food) are provided, which the children use to act out stories alone or with peers. In the types of imaginative play scenarios described here, children invent characters, dialogue, and action.

In doing so, they practice and expand their oral language skills. The dramas performed by the teacher are a very effective way to communicate scientific information. At the same time, important listening skills are developed. Children at all developmental levels of language learning can follow along because the drama is presented using realistic props. As they listen, children are processing new information and integrating it into their existing cognitive frameworks.

PEACHES also incorporates language arts into the curriculum by including literature in the units. Each guide contains a "Literature Connections" section with recommendations of books that complement the activities. There are also suggestions for language experience activities such as making class books.

Science and Language for Children with Limited English Skills

Teachers who incorporate science activities from the GEMS/PEACHES units observe that children with limited English language skills can readily communicate with English-speaking children through hands-on science and math investigations.

A 4-year-old child with limited English language skills was very shy and withdrawn from the regular curriculum activities performed in the classroom. However, when I was building a terrarium and bringing a few snails to live inside it, he got very excited and began to smile. He grabbed the hand of a friend (who only spoke English) and made a gesture of looking for snails in the playground. The two kids became very close through their common interest—looking for small animals to live in the terrarium. Every day they brought different animals such as ants, pill bugs, earthworms, ladybugs, and snails for the terrarium. By the end of the year, it was clear their friendship would outlast the experimental world they had created in the terrarium."

During the *Tree Homes* activity, in which children observe a tree, a Spanish-speaking child learned not only the concept of tree, but also bark, soil, leaves, flowers, texture, rough, and soft. This experience was clearly more concrete than simply translating or showing pictures of trees."

— *Patricia House*

The activities enable children to understand aspects of science that relate to their daily lives. Children are encouraged to make their own sensory observations and to devise their own experiments. They can learn about organisms and the physical world firsthand without needing to know the concepts in English beforehand.

After children with limited English skills directly participate in an activity, rather than just memorizing a translated version, bilingual teachers can then stimulate the children to increase their English language and thinking skills by building on the vocabulary and ideas that naturally stem from the science activity.

Because the PEACHES approach weaves science and math into a rich tapestry of dramatic arts, crafts, play, and sensory exploration, children with limited English gain new knowledge and skills while fully taking part in the group discovery process.

Chapter 6   Equity and Excellence in Early Childhood Education

On average, an early childhood program in the United States today is ethnically, culturally, and linguistically more diverse than at any other time in our history. Researchers predict that by 2001 no one group in California will be in the "majority," so every group will be a "minority!" By 2050 this will be the case for the United States as a whole.

Within this multicultural framework, one of the most important goals of mathematics and science education is to build toward an educational system that can provide opportunities for **all** students to achieve success. As the *National Science Education Standards* put it:

> *The intent of the Standards can be expressed in a single phrase: Science standards for all students. The phrase embodies both excellence and equity. The Standards apply to all students, regardless of age, gender, cultural or ethnic background, disabilities, aspirations, or interest and motivation in science . . .*

Mathematics educators have long been at the forefront of equity issues, advocating the need to provide mathematical opportunities to all students, and emphasizing mathematics as a gateway to higher education that has historically been denied to underrepresented groups. This emphasis on equity and access is continuing, as the National Council of Teachers of Mathematics (NCTM) prepares its *Principles and Standards for School Mathematics* which highlights equity as the first of six main principles.

In early childhood education, striving for equity and excellence means ensuring that each and every child has a high-quality, challenging, culturally relevant, non-biased, safe, and nonthreatening learning environment. Such an environment should offer numerous opportunities for each child to learn, grow, express herself in a variety of ways, and reach her own unique level of understanding and excellence.

Early childhood educators and their organizations, such as the National Association for the Education of Young Children (NAEYC), have long embraced goals related to equity and access. NAEYC's Code of Ethical Conduct states:

> *Standards of professional practice in early childhood programs are based on commitment to certain fundamental values that are deeply rooted in the history of the early childhood field:*
>
> - *appreciating childhood as a unique and valuable stage of the human life cycle;*
>
> - *basing our work with children on knowledge of child development and learning;*
>
> - *appreciating and supporting the close ties between the child and family;*
>
> - *recognizing that children are best understood in the context of family, culture, and society;*
>
> - *respecting the dignity, worth, and uniqueness of each individual; and*

- *helping children and adults achieve their full potential in the context of relationships that are based on trust, respect, and positive regard.*

Early childhood educators are among the most powerful and persuasive in implementing programs designed to reach all students, emphasize positive multicultural values, and foster respect for the multiplicity of cultures, backgrounds, languages, abilities, and learning styles in our society.

Gender Equity

Over the past several decades, women have made significant progress on many fronts. The women's movement has had a profound impact on education, and larger numbers of women are attending colleges and universities and going on to advanced work than ever before. In the fields of mathematics and science, more women than ever are entering careers formerly closed to them, both in the United States and in much of the rest of the world.

Despite social and legal advances, economic discrimination, such as differential pay for the same work, remains a fact of life. Women are still underrepresented, not only in scientific, mathematical, and technical fields, but in many other professional categories. In the classroom, studies show many teachers unconsciously reinforce stereotypical gender roles in their assumptions, class management, and assignments. Even when teachers are aware of such studies, and/or consciously set out to treat boys and girls equally, analysis of what they actually do often reveals how such bias is persistent and culturally reinforced.

The NCTM book, *Multicultural and Gender Equity in the Mathematics Classroom: The Gift of Diversity*, contains articles on these issues, including "Uncovering Bias in the Classroom—A Personal Journey" in which a teacher examines her own classroom practice.

As with so much else, parental influences and educational practices regarding gender roles can have a profound impact on a child's entire life direction. It is important for early childhood educators and parents to be aware of how formative early experiences are. Even if a woman teacher has a dislike or fear of insects ("Little Miss Muffet, sat on a tuffet") she should try not to pass on that attitude to her students! By the same token, the caring and tender side of learning how to handle and treat classroom animals or pets at home should be encouraged in both boys and girls.

It shouldn't be assumed girls will be less interested in computers or building blocks. When activities are structured in a flexible way that allows for students to exercise their natural curiosity and inquiry, both girls and boys find plenty of fascination in a wide range of activities. You my find it helpful to have girls work together at block-building or computer stations. Remember, the seeds of science and mathematics are planted early—to cut off a sprout of interest due to gender stereotyping is to deprive the child of all the possibilities that might flower in the future.

There are a number of educational programs and organizations throughout the country that concentrate on attaining a higher standard of gender equity in education. At the Lawrence Hall of Science, programs such as EQUALS and Family Math make important contributions to these efforts by designing activities and materials aimed at promoting the full involvement and participation of girls/young women and other historically underrepresented groups in mathematics and science education.

Many other LHS programs focus on important audiences of inclusion, such as English-language learners and students with physical disabilities. Programs such as GEMS and PEACHES are designed to reach and motivate all students. Written for teachers without a special background in math and science, utilizing everyday materials, and tested widely with diverse populations in many regions, accessibility is one of our main goals. In development and testing, in photographs and language, careful attention is paid to ensuring the full participation of girls and young women.

Connections with Many Cultures

A learning environment needs to be culturally relevant. Children should be able to see their own culture, as well as the vibrancy of other cultures, represented and reflected in a positive and in-depth way in their surroundings through books, photos, posters, and curricula. It's fine to observe African-American history month or Chinese New Year, but awareness and knowledge of diverse cultures should encompass much more. It's important not to take an oversimplified route to such cultural exploration by depicting certain aspects in a superficial or stereotypical way. A good way to avoid this is to go to the source—invite a parent or group of parents to share something significant about their culture with the class. Have them emphasize those traditions that are common to all—celebrations of the seasons, life-stages, family, harvest, earth's resources.

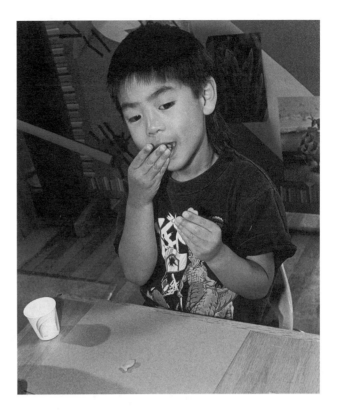

Everyone benefits from the experience. It strengthens the ties between the home and school as well as those between parents and teacher. It validates their home culture for the particular parents and their children. Other children and families in the class are introduced to the richness of another culture.

There are many excellent curricula that focus directly on cultural diversity. In *Investigating Artifacts*, children learn a great deal about diverse Native American and world cultures, and in *Eggs Eggs Everywhere*, children and parents are invited to share egg traditions with their class. The "Literature Connections" of GEMS/PEACHES units emphasize the many excellent books that explore different cultures in respectful ways. Cooperative learning and collaborative problem solving, which are a key part of all GEMS/PEACHES activities, are among the best ways to both bridge and appreciate differences and diversities in culture and background.

Relevant connections also need to be made to the child's real-life experiences. This makes learning meaningful for children by relating what is being taught to their experiences at home and in their communities.

In *The Dreamkeepers: Successful Teachers of African American Children,* author Gloria Ladson-Billings points out some characteristics of teachers with culturally relevant practices and looks at outcomes of culturally relevant teaching. In her view, teachers with culturally relevant practices have a high regard for others, believe all children can succeed, help children make connections between their community, national, and global identities, and see teaching as "digging knowledge out" of children.

Language and Culture

One of the most significant aspects of culture is language. Today, it is estimated that more than one in five children in early childhood programs speaks a language other than English at home. This ratio is expected to increase to one in three over the next 10 to 20 years. In a classroom of 20

children, it is conceivable that one might find nearly that many different home languages!

Any child in a new environment may feel lonely, isolated, and fearful at first. This can be especially true of children who do not speak the language used in the classroom. The NAEYC emphasizes that ties between family and early childhood programs are strengthened when educators acknowledge and respect all children's home languages and cultures, and encourage and promote the active involvement and support of all families, including extended and nontraditional family units. Researchers find knowing more than one language is a cognitive asset, and the development of a child's home language does not interfere with the ability to learn English. A child learns any language best in the context of meaningful, day-to-day interactions with adults or other children who speak that language.

Activity-based mathematics and science provides those meaningful day-to-day interactions and can serve as an outstanding and effective platform for English-language learners, as well as fostering the literacy skills of all students.

Learning Styles

Children's pathways to learning differ. Multidisciplinary and multisensory ways of approaching learning can provide effective ways to reach students with diverse learning styles.

We are all capable of all types of learning, and we all utilize different combinations of these learning styles or learning modalities. Different individuals have different strengths and preferences. While it may often be best to present information to a student that complements her learning style, it can also be extremely important to provide ways for her to better develop her abilities through other modes of learning as well.

- A **visual learner,** after hearing an explanation or when presented with new or confusing concepts, responds with "Just show me!"

- A **tactile learner** wants to touch, feel, and manipulate objects.

- An **auditory learner** gains understanding from what is heard.

- A **kinesthetic learner** uses bodily control and movement to express himself.

Multiple Intelligences

In his 1983 book, *Frames of Mind,* Harvard psychologist Howard Gardner put forward a theory of "multiple intelligences." Since then, his ideas have been widely discussed among educators. According to Gardner, all humans possesses *at least* seven intelligences. Those intelligences, Gardner says, have to do with the capacity for solving problems and the ability to fashion products or creations in a complex real-life setting. In attempting to integrate the findings of modern brain science and psychology, Gardner sees "intelligence" as a biological and psychological **potential**— capable of being realized to a greater or lesser extent depending on one's experience, education, social environment, and other factors. Gardner's seven intelligences are:

- **Linguistic Intelligence**
  The capacity to use words effectively, orally or in writing. This intelligence includes the ability to manipulate the structure and syntax of language, the sounds of language, semantics or the meanings of language, and the practical uses of language, such as for explaining, remembering, persuading.

- **Logical-Mathematical Intelligence**
  The capacity to use numbers effectively and to reason well. This intelligence includes awareness of logical patterns and relationships, functions, and cause and effect statements.

- **Spatial Intelligence**
  The ability to perceive the visual and spatial world accurately, and to engage in processes based on those perceptions, including sensitivity to color, line, shape, form, space, and the relationships between them. This intelligence includes the capacity to visualize, make graphic representations, and orient oneself in spatial surroundings.

- **Bodily-Kinesthetic Intelligence**
  The ability to use one's whole body to express ideas and feelings, and the ability to fashion or transform with one's hands. This intelligence includes skills such as coordination, balance, dexterity, strength, flexibility, speed, and other physical skills.

- **Musical Intelligence**
  The ability to perceive, distinguish between, transform, and express oneself in musical forms. This intelligence includes sensitivities to rhythm, pitch or melody, timbre and tone color; and can include either an intuitive grasp of music, an analytic or technical understanding of it, or both.

- **Interpersonal Intelligence**
  The capacity to perceive and distinguish differences in the moods, intentions, motiva-

tions, and feelings of others. This intelligence includes sensitivity to facial expressions, gestures, and body language. It also includes the ability to respond to these interpersonal cues effectively, to work well with others, and to lead.

- **Intrapersonal Intelligence**
  The capacity for self-knowledge and understanding, and the ability to act on the basis of that knowledge. This intelligence includes having an accurate picture of one's own strengths and limitations, inner moods, intentions, feelings, motivations, needs, desires, and a capacity for self-discipline and self-esteem.

Gardner and others emphasize that the exact number of "intelligences" is less important than the idea that there are many kinds. In recent articles, Gardner discusses an eighth intelligence, which he calls the *Naturalist Intelligence:* "It seems to me that the individual who is able readily to recognize flora and fauna, to make other distinctions in the natural world, and to use this ability productively is exercising an important intelligence and one that is not adequately encompassed on the current list."

(For fuller descriptions of these complex ideas, we recommend Gardner's books as well as books by Thomas Armstrong on applying multiple intelligences in the classroom. Please see References on page 77.)

GEMS/PEACHES units are highly responsive to these ideas. In *Tree Homes*, for example, students take part in dramas and other forms of oral expression *(linguistic intelligence);* they match holes in trees with shapes and consider how to categorize bears *(logical/mathematical intelligence);* they make models, view posters, and work with a three-dimensional tree model *(spatial intelligence);* take part in an activity where they snuggle together *(bodily-kinesthetic intelligence);* engage in small group and whole class activities *(interpersonal intelligence);* make their own models and use props independently in dramas *(intrapersonal intelligence);* and go outside to observe real trees, sort and classify bears *(naturalist intelligence).*

It is important to emphasize, as Gardner does, that all of us possess all of these intelligences in varying combinations and strengths. His goal is not to analyze people from the standpoint of how much of a particular intelligence they possess, but to cause people to recognize that there are many powerful and creative kinds of intelligence in addition to the linguistic and mathematical abilities measured on standard intelligence tests, or college boards, and traditionally described in school as being "smart." As Gardner says, "It's not how smart you are, but *how* you are smart!"

In response to ideas about multiple intelligences and diverse learning styles, as well as related findings in current brain and cognitive research, the PEACHES curriculum and GEMS units incorporate multisensory, multidisciplinary approaches to learning that allow all types of learners to grow and learn, and to express themselves in a multitude of ways.

The combination of understanding and emphasis on science and mathematics for all students, along with gender equity, cultural relevance, multicultural respect, language acquisition, learning styles, and multiple intelligences can lead us towards the twin goals of equity and excellence in education.

Chapter 7 Mathematics in Early Childhood

Ask a roomful of adults to think back on their mathematics education, and you are likely to hear them recall memories of lots of computational work, word problems, timed tests, and the quest for the "right" answer. This emphasis on number work painted a monochromatic image of mathematics. Now, tell those same adults that they use mathematics in their daily lives—when they estimate the cost of their groceries, modify a recipe, plant a garden, schedule car pools, arrange storage space, or evaluate the statistical claims behind a product. They may be surprised to see that the mathematics they are doing goes well beyond the limited scope they remember from their school experience!

Everyday Mathematics

Mathematics is an integral part of young children's daily experiences. As children put puzzle pieces together (spatial sense), explore treasure items (sorting and classifying), build with blocks (work with three-dimensional shapes), count out cookies for a snack (number sense), put toys away (sorting), and follow routines (pattern), they are developing an understanding of mathematics concepts through everyday play and activities. Adults can enhance these opportunities by asking questions that promote discussion of mathematical ideas. Although this type of learning is informal, it is very powerful and develops a child's mathematical foundation. During these early years, it is also important to introduce the language and conventions of mathematics. Books, songs, and finger-plays are engaging ways for children to learn mathematics vocabulary and counting skills, as well as develop spatial sense. Things to count, sort, compare, match, put together and take apart should also be accessible to young

children. At the preschool and all levels, mathematics should involve more than numbers.

Once children enter kindergarten, their intuitive and informal mathematics knowledge can be extended though concrete experiences. Using real-world contexts, mathematics concepts and skills can be developed. The learning environment should encourage active participation and reflect children's natural interests. From kindergarten through second grade, children experience profound developmental change. It is important to keep in mind that children develop at different rates and in different ways. However, regardless of where children are in their development, they need to build positive beliefs about themselves as **mathematics learners** to ensure future success.

Mathematics Across the Curriculum

Children's interest and curiosity in the natural world provides a wonderful context to develop mathematical concepts. The GEMS/PEACHES early childhood units lend themselves to meaningful integration of mathematics and science along with language, literature, art, music, and drama. The mathematics content in these guides includes number, geometry and spatial sense, measurement, pattern, statistics and prob-

ability, and problem solving. Concepts and skills are developed through hands-on, real-world activities. By making mathematics meaningful and teaching it in context, a foundation is established for children's mathematics learning so it can be further built upon throughout a child's education. The mathematics content for a rich early childhood program is outlined next with examples from the GEMS/PEACHES guides.

Number

Number is fundamental to all aspects of mathematics. Numbers are used to define quantities and relationships, to measure, to make comparisons, to interpret information, and to solve problems. Beginning with concrete, real-world experiences, numbers are understood by counting "how many" and measuring "how much." Number sense is developed over time by representing numbers in different ways, understanding relationships among numbers, and understanding operations and place value.

Some Examples of
— GEMS/PEACHES CONNECTIONS —

- *Ant Homes Under the Ground*
  Buzzing A Hive
  Ladybugs

  In each of these units, children create models of insects, each with three body parts, six legs, and two antennae. This process provides counting practice as well as physical representations of three numbers. It also lays the foundation for categorizing animals by their physical structures. In *Ant Homes Under the Ground*, by using a model of an ant nest, children use counting and computational skills to fill the ant hill.

- *Frog Math*
  Children develop their estimation skills and use a place value board as a counting tool.

- *Penguins and Their Young*
  As children play a game that simulates penguin behavior, they add and subtract concretely using crackers.

- *Treasure Boxes*
  Children create "fair shares" of treasure items and develop an understanding of division.

- *Mother Opossum and Her Babies*
  The pockets on children's clothing are used in connection with an opossum's pouch for an estimation and counting activity that uses place value.

Geometry and Spatial Sense

Geometry connects us to the real world—everything has a shape or form. From their earliest days, children explore shapes and structures in their environment. As their language develops, they learn the names and characteristics of two- and three-dimensional shapes. As they compare shapes, they can recognize congruent and similar shapes. They also develop spatial sense as they build, give and follow directions, navigate objects and themselves, and put things together and take them apart. At this developmental stage they can investigate special topics in geometry such as symmetry.

Some Examples of
— GEMS/PEACHES CONNECTIONS —

- *Penguins and Their Young*
  Children watch frozen, three-dimensional geometric shapes melt in a tub of water.

- *Eggs Eggs Everywhere*
  Children discover what objects, by shape, will roll down a ramp.

- *Tree Homes*
  In making a cardboard tree model, children use large cardboard boxes in three sizes and cut ellipses in them for the tree holes.

  Children perform an owl finger-play to develop spatial sense through drama and movement activities.

- *Buzzing A Hive*
  As children investigate beehives they learn about hexagons.

- *Build It! Festival*
  Children explore two- and three-dimensional shapes to identify characteristics and name the shapes. The unit provides opportunities to explore patterns, number, and symmetry.

- *Treasure Boxes*
  Children learn to use a coordinate grid as they play a treasure hunt game.

- *Ladybugs*
  While making ladybugs, children explore bilateral symmetry in ladybugs and familiar classroom objects, as well as through art projects.

  - *Ant Homes Under the Ground*
    To develop spatial sense through drama and movement activities, children simulate ant behavior and crawl through an ant tunnel. They sort and classify ants using the attribute of shape to categorize the ants.

  - *Frog Math*
    Children use the attribute of shape to categorize and graph buttons.

Measurement

Measurement is also strongly connected to our everyday lives. Whoever cooks or orders takeout food needs to know about quantities. Likewise, those who drive cars have to know about capacity—they've learned how far they can go before the gauge hits the "E" mark! Length, capacity, weight, area, mass, volume, time, temperature, and money are all aspects of daily life that make use of measurement.

For young children, measurement begins with comparisons—which item is bigger? who has the most? what is heavier? Children love to compare themselves to everything! When they begin to measure real objects and events, nonstandard, familiar items (toothpicks, wooden cubes) can be used as a measuring tool as can non-uniform, nonstandard units of measurement (hand-spans or foot lengths). Using these tools, they learn the technique of measuring lengths and areas. Once the measurement is taken and quantified, comparisons can be made. Questions such as "How long is each item?" "Which item is longer?" "How much longer?" can then be answered. As measurement skills and understanding grow, measuring tools can be expanded to include a standard unit of measurement such as a ruler.

Some Examples of
— GEMS/PEACHES CONNECTIONS —

- *Penguins and Their Young*
  Children compare their height to that of an Emperor penguin.

- *Sifting Through Science*
  When working with magnets, children compare the relative strengths of each magnet.

- *Liquid Explorations*
  Children compare the similarities and differences between oil and water.

- *Mother Opossum and Her Babies*
  Children make a hand print next to an opossum paw print to compare size and structure. Children measure the length of a life-size mother opossum with familiar, nonstandard objects. They make a model of a young opossum and compare its length to objects in their environment.

- *Tree Homes*
  When sorting toy bears, the children discuss and name the various sizes of bears from "teeny-tiny" to gigantic, and then group them accordingly. The model tree home's holes serve as a measurement tool and are used to determine which animals can fit within each size hole.

- *Bubble Festival*

   As children blow bubbles, they try to create the largest bubble possible and measure bubbles with nonstandard items.

- *Secret Formulas*

   Children use nonstandard tools to measure and record quantities.

Patterns

Patterns are everywhere—in nature, art, science, music, history—and they are at the heart of mathematics. A pattern can be found in anything that repeats itself over and over. Starting at a young age, children experience pattern when going about daily routines, doing activities that involve repetitive sequences (such as songs, finger-plays, rhythmic clapping), and by finding patterns in their environment. Building on these experiences, children learn to identify, analyze and extend patterns. Looking for patterns is an important problem-solving strategy, and patterns help children develop the ability to form generalizations.

Some Examples of
— GEMS/PEACHES CONNECTIONS —

- *Build It! Festival*

   Children discern and extend patterns with pattern blocks and use the blocks to fill tessellation patterns.

- *Ladybugs*

   Children make a life cycle book that concretely illustrates the ladybug's life cycle.

- *Buzzing A Hive*

   Bee posters illustrate the bee's life cycle. Children look for patterns when they simulate bees doing a bee dance.

- *Tree Homes*

   Children learn a rhythmic owl finger-play with a repeating verse.

- *Frog Math*

   Number patterns are a key strategy to winning the "Frog Pond" game.

Statistics and Probability

Data and statistics abound in our daily lives—from opinion polls to the annual rainfall in your local area. Statistics are generated in many ways, including surveys, experiments, sports, polls, demographics, and observations. The field of statistics involves the collection, classification, analysis, and interpretation of data. The data are represented, for example, in the form of tables, graphs, and charts.

To begin to develop an understanding of statistics, children benefit from experiences that allow them to organize data and make sense out of it. As a preliminary step to organizing data, children need experience sorting and classifying, counting, and comparing. Graphs are a key tool to organize and represent data so it can be analyzed. The interpretation of data can range from identifying quantities (six red shoes) to comparing the data on the graph (there are more black shoes). Children benefit by seeing the same data organized in different ways so they can see how it can convey different information. For example, shoes can be organized by color or size, which provides different information about the shoes.

Though young children are not ready to explore theoretical probability, there are aspects of probability that are developmentally appropriate. Probability involves predictions or guesses. Children can predict the likelihood of an event happening. In addition, they can conduct informal probability experiments through games using coins, dice, and spinners, and keep track of the outcomes. This gives them an intuitive understanding on which to build concepts in theoretical probability, which they will investigate in later grades.

Some Examples of
— GEMS/PEACHES CONNECTIONS —

- *Eggs Eggs Everywhere*
  Children open toy eggs and discover a wealth of miniature egg-laying animals that they sort and classify. After sorting these animals, students create a concrete graph with them and make observations about the data.

- *Frog Math*
  After sorting real buttons, children craft paper buttons and organize these buttons on a bar graph in a variety of ways. Children play games using dice and acquire an understanding about the frequency with which certain numbers occur.

- *Sifting Through Science*
  The data from hands-on experiments is organized on concrete graphs to help interpret the findings. Children also create pictorial graphs to record the information.

- *Investigating Artifacts*
  Children sort natural objects they find and then create masks, which can be sorted and classified by characteristics.

- *Treasure Boxes*
  The treasure items are sorted in a variety of ways and children are given an open-ended graphing grid to organize the items. They are encouraged to make observations about the graphs in the form of "true statements," using numbers and comparisons.

- *Ant Homes Under the Ground*
  Data is collected informally as children observe ants in the outdoor environment and their classroom over time. These activities allow students to make predictions about what will happen on an ongoing basis.

- *Terrarium Habitats*
  Children observe and can record data about what is happening over time. These activities allow students to make predictions about what will happen on an ongoing basis.

Problem Solving

Problem solving involves analytic thinking and reasoning. Young children are natural problem-solvers who approach challenges with a positive attitude. In the process of solving problems, they develop strategies that can be applied to new situations. The process by which they solve problems is as important as their solutions. Students need encouragement and support in articulating the processes they use to reach solutions to problems. In addition, they need assistance identifying different problem-solving strategies to develop a "tool kit" they can use when they approach new situations.

The problems posed for young children need to have a real-world context so they have meaning and a reason to solve them for children. In addition, children should have many opportunities to solve a variety of problems that focus on different strategies. Children should see that many problems have more than one solution and evaluate which solution or solutions is best to use to solve a particular problem.

Problems that help develop mathematical content need to be embedded in the rest of the curriculum as well. For problem solving to permeate the mathematics program and other curricula, it is best nurtured in an environment that supports exchange of ideas, questioning, and investigations.

Some Examples of
— GEMS/PEACHES CONNECTIONS —

• *Group Solutions*
Group Solutions, Too!
> Both these guides are filled with logic problems to be solved by children working cooperatively to arrive at solutions. Mathematics content is embedded in each problem, and children have a chance to develop and practice deductive reasoning, process of elimination, and communication skills.

• *Frog Math*
> The Frog Pond game is an adaptation of NIM, an ancient Chinese logic game. As students play this game, they develop and refine logical-thinking skills as they experiment with different strategies to win the game.

• *Animal Defenses*
> Using problem-solving skills, children apply what they know about animal defenses to craft a protected animal from a defenseless animal form.

• *Investigating Artifacts*
> Children uncover clues from the past as they explore a simulated midden. They use their problem-solving skills to create a story behind the artifacts they find.

• *Build It! Festival*
> Children find multiple solutions to geometric problems, ranging from filling shapes with blocks to constructing stable three-dimensional shapes. As they work, they use a variety of problem-solving strategies and share solutions.

MORE NATIONAL MATHEMATICS STANDARDS

As children actively learn mathematics content, attention should be paid to developing their ability to reason, communicate their thinking, make connections, and create representations. The four standards ("Reasoning and Proof," "Connections," "Representation," and "Communications") emphasize instructional practices rather than content, and are embedded in all six content standards.

Reasoning and Proof

Children have an innate belief that the world is supposed to make sense. Early experiences with mathematical reasoning support and nurture sense-making by developing children's ability to think clearly and check new ideas against what is known. Key elements in this process are pattern recognition and classification skills. Concrete experiences help children develop clear and precise thought processes. This development goes hand-in-glove with the their language development. To support the development of reasoning, children need opportunities to justify their thinking and develop logical arguments.

Communication

Communication plays a vital role in gaining mathematical literacy. Children express what they know in a variety of ways including with concrete materials, drawings, diagrams, writing, and verbal communication. And when they listen to other children and the teacher, alternative perspectives and strategies are communicated that enhance mathematical understanding. Representations, discussions, writing, and reading can also share mathematical content and processes. As children's knowledge and vocabulary increases, the use of precise mathematical language and conventional mathematical symbolism provides a universal vehicle to express mathematical ideas. Language—both written and oral—is a powerful tool that fosters the learning and communication of math.

Connections

To make mathematics more meaningful, children need opportunities to see the connections among mathematical ideas as well as see the ways math is used outside of mathematics. Fortunately, young children experience mathematics as a part of their world in organic ways, such as counting the steps of a staircase, creating patterns in art, identifying the beats in music, and counting legs on insects. Often children provide mathematical teaching opportunities by their interests, questions, and observations. Teachers are the facilitators who capitalize on these teachable moments to connect different areas of mathematics to each other and to the real world.

Representation

Representations provide insight into a child's grasp of mathematical concepts. Young children represent their mathematical ideas and procedures in many ways—using their fingers or manipulatives, orally, or with idiosyncratic symbols, drawings, diagrams, and dramatizations. Children naturally represent their mathematical ideas using their own methods. These representations reveal a great deal about their thinking and often resemble more formal representations. Through interactions with these external representations, children begin to develop their own mental images of mathematical ideas. Teachers should provide as many different representations as needed to help children gain mathematical understanding. It is important for students and teachers to realize that any representation, whether made by children or adults, is subject to multiple interpretations.

Chapter 8 Timely Questions

Questions make up a big part of our daily conversations at school and at home with families and friends. Good questions can promote observations and encourage children to share their ideas. A simple question such as "What do you see happening in the terrarium?" can focus attention on an important process that might be overlooked. A question such as "How are the snails and slugs similar?" stimulates children to compare and contrast the properties of organisms and objects. Questions can be pow-

erful tools for stimulating children to think, describe, and ask questions of their own.

"What kind of animal is shown in this picture?" is a question that requires children to recall a specific piece of information. This narrow kind of question can be useful at the beginning of an activity to get children thinking about a topic that has been interrupted, or as part of a closing discussion to solidify vocabulary. Too often we overuse these "test-like" questions that

require children to recite facts. Consider the following broader question: "What might happen if you put a tiny piece of paper in this spider's web?" This invitation to speculate on spider behavior will stimulate interesting ideas and vocabulary. It has the added benefit of posing a problem that can be tested by the children.

Divergent and Convergent Questions

Questions can be *divergent* or *convergent*. Divergent questions, such as the spider web question, do not have one right answer but provide an opportunity for creativity, guessing, and experimenting. Divergent questions stretch children's thinking.

"What do you think?"

"What did you find out?"

"What might happen if?"

"How can you make this object roll?"

Convergent questions ask for specific information, such as "How many legs does a spider have?" While these questions provide us with feedback on what children recall, when used too often, convergent questions can limit a child's thinking and willingness to guess and experiment.

We gain valuable information by listening to children's responses to questions—their ideas may lead an activity into new and interesting directions! The following are some techniques for using divergent and convergent questions productively.

- Ask questions that require more than a "yes" or "no" response. Compare "Have you seen a ladybug before?" to questions such as "Where have you seen ladybugs?" "What were they doing?" The latter questions invite the child to think about relationships and interactions between living things.

- After you ask a question, give the children time to think before taking responses. Wait a few seconds to give the children time to ponder and formulate their ideas.

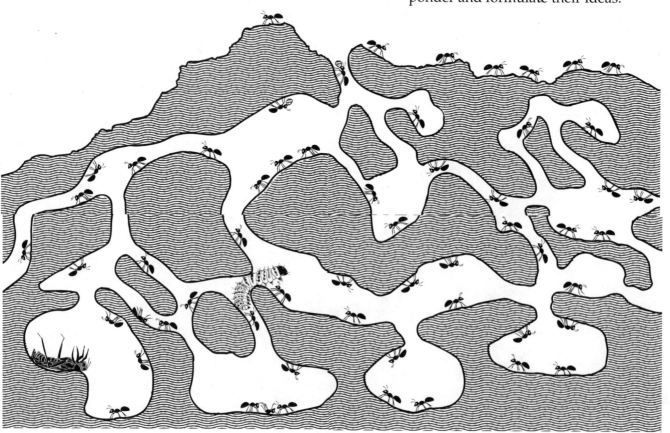

- Ask children for their ideas about the subject. With the simple addition of the phrase "What do you think?" a convergent question becomes centered on the child's ideas and predictions rather than on a particular right answer. "What do you think will happen if we put this water in the freezer?" invites discussion in a more friendly way than "What will happen if we put this water in the freezer?"

- Ask questions with more than one answer and questions that promote investigation. This encourages many children to contribute to the discussion.

    "What kinds of animals might come to a pond for a drink of water?"

    "What do you predict will happen if we let go of this ball at the top of the ramp?"

  These divergent questions encourage descriptions, comparisons, and predictions.

- Posters and drawings can become more effective teaching tools when used with a series of questions. Using the poster in *Ant Homes Under the Ground*, here are some convergent questions that could be asked.

    "What kinds of jobs are the ants doing?"

    "How many ants are walking upside down?"

    "What other kinds of animals are in the ant hill?"

    "Where is the largest ant?"

- While children are engaged with investigations, use divergent questions to find out what they are thinking.

    "Where have you seen ants?"

    "What might cause the ants to change their trail?"

    "What might happen if food is put near the ant hill?"

    "How do you think ants help the forest?"

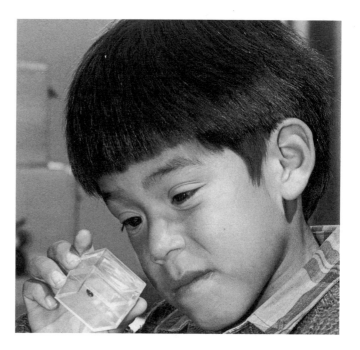

Open-Ended Questions

Asking open-ended questions is a wonderful way for many children to respond without hesitation. Most everyone has an opinion when they are asked, "What do you like about ___?" or "Why do you think the worms moved to this end?" Sometimes we need to ask convergent questions that require a specific answer. Frequently children's responses are incorrect! Wrong answers should be acknowledged to support the child in his or her effort to respond. Restating the question may help redirect the child's thinking. "That's a good guess; let's look at all the ants again to find the biggest one."

All answers, correct and incorrect, are an opportunity for adults to evaluate children's understanding and experience with a particular topic or activity. Finding out *why* a question was answered in a certain way may be more important than the response being "right" or "wrong." Encouraging children to explain their reasoning, in cases of both "right" and "wrong" answers can provide important insight into their thinking, help identify misconceptions they may have, as well as help them improve their oral expression and ability to communicate.

Why Is the Sky Blue?

What about children's questions you can't answer? We try to be prepared, but youngsters frequently ask unexpected questions. If the scope of the question goes beyond your experience, tell the children that you don't know, and suggest ways you might find the answer together. Adults should not attempt to be the source of all answers, but instead should help children investigate their own questions. By presenting it as a "let's find out together" venture you are encouraging cooperation and teaching children to be resourceful.

The question "Why is the sky blue?" can be rephrased to promote an investigation. "What are some colors you have seen in the sky?" can be

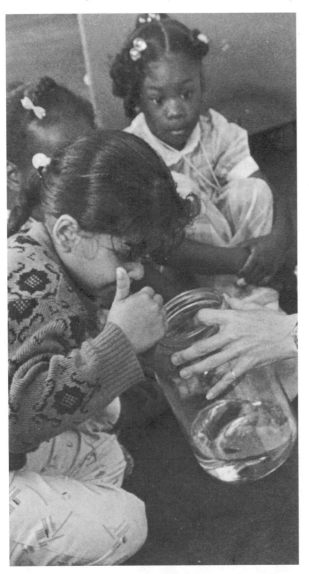

the starting point for daily observations and descriptions of weather. "What is happening when the sky isn't blue?" becomes an important and observable part of the child's findings. Many homes and schools have plastic prisms hanging in windows. These delightful light separators can become part of the investigation. Eventually "blue sky" will be just one part of a rich and tangible "Sky Study" created by the children.

By avoiding the complex physics explanation of blue sky, you teach children they can find out answers to things they wonder about. If you then decide to read an explanation of blue sky from a science book, present the information in a way that validates their findings as curious and avid young scientists.

Whenever possible, rephrase difficult "why" and "how" questions into ones that can be investigated by the children. Don't try to explain density to youngsters who ask "Why does this float?" Give them lots of different objects to test and ask questions such as:

> "Which objects are floaters and which are sinkers?"
> "In what ways are floaters and sinkers similar?"
> "Can you make a sinker float?"
> "Tell me what you know about things that float."

Children who play with and investigate objects in water will not understand and cannot explain the physics of buoyancy—the concept is too abstract. They will however become adept at predicting the behavior of objects in water, and their explanations about why they designed their boats in certain ways will be closely tied to their observations.

We invite you to take a closer look at how you use questions and the nature of children's responses. As you experiment with using questions that are open-ended and accessible to youngsters, you will gain insights into their reasoning.

Please see Resources Related to Questions on page 80 for helpful references on the productive use of questions.

Chapter 9 Active Assessment

Assessment means many things to different people. But for those of us working with young children, assessment is finding out what children know so they can continue to learn and do so in better ways. Therefore, assessment is an important tool for teachers, as it informs our instructional practices and curriculum, and allows us to adapt and modify our program to the changing needs of our children. Ultimately, we want to help children become evaluators of their own learning so that the spark to continue discovering and inquiring comes from within rather than from external indicators such as grades or "rewards." If we can do that, we have contributed to the development of life-long learners who are not afraid to reflect on what they know and pursue what they want to know more about.

The drive to learn and be successful is innate in all of us. Parents and educators often comment on the power of this quest for knowledge and skill mastery in their youngsters. Given encouragement and a nurturing environment, children explore, test things, ask questions, and try out new pathways in their search for answers.

At the heart of parenting and teaching is the question—how do we know children are learning what we want them to learn?

Preschool teachers and parents from around the country explored that question during several PEACHES Summer Institutes sponsored by the National Science Foundation. In observing children using new information and skills, they came up with lots of things to look for to determine if children did indeed learn what was being taught. The participants were surprised by the great variety of behaviors youngsters exhibit that can be used to assess their ideas, attitudes, skills, and knowledge.

Things to look for include the following:

- Children's own reports of their learning.

- Use of the new vocabulary.

- Spontaneous recognition of something they've learned (surprise in their faces, exclamations, pointing).

- Correcting incorrect information.

- Bringing in their own knowledge to make comparisons.

- Responses to questions.

- Recording observations; making journals.

- Physical coordination in movement, speech, and song.

- Use of various skills and equipment to measure, build, and create.

- Assisting other children to learn what they've learned.

- Creating representations—constructing models, drawing pictures, sculpting objects, building structures, rearranging materials, and acting out dramas.

- Talking and playing with others about what they've learned.

- Spending time investigating and seeking more information.

- Responses during problem-solving activities: successful grouping, matching, recognition of relationships such as geometric shapes, logical thinking, strategies for solution.

Opossums hang their babies under their bodies in a pouch.

Brian

Some Methods of Assessment

There are a number of methods you can use to assess your children's learning.

- **Keep a portfolio of each student's work, along with notes and observations.**

  A portfolio for each child chronicling the student's activity through the year could contain items such as projects, self portraits, and literacy indicators—dictated stories and journals, photographs, audio/video tapes of interviews and activity sessions. These portfolios and notes can be used in a very positive way to show children and their parents the richness of the student's learning and progress.

- **Pre-evaluate the student's knowledge.**

  For example, before starting investigations of soil organisms, a teacher gave children the opportunity to investigate a tray of soil. By asking open-ended questions such as "What might live in this?" and "What do you notice about this?" the teacher learned about the interests, fears, and knowledge the children brought to the activity.

- **Post-evaluate the student's knowledge.**

  In post-evaluation interviews you may find the children using new vocabulary and information, and showing greater enthusiasm.

- **Keep a summary of progress.**

  A summary of progress could include areas such as skill development, attitudes, and literacy development. You may want to keep the summaries in the form of a checklist to indicate progress towards acquisition of a skill or behavior. These periodic summaries are valuable for getting an overall measure of progress.

Assessment needs to be a natural part of ongoing routines so you can respond quickly to the needs and interests of the children. Parents and teachers may find this approach improves their own observation skills and provides exciting insights into their children's learning.

Standardized methods are commonly used to assess youngsters' learning and to make comparisons to grade-level norms for this age group. Educators are concerned that the progress of young children tends to be undervalued by literacy-based systems of evaluation. Factual knowledge, emphasized by many assessment systems, is only one realm of what a child knows and is learning.

The development of ideas often comes about through detours, explorations, and making connections. An experiment or experience that yields unexpected results (sometimes called a discrepant event) can be a particularly powerful way for children to confront some of their old ideas and wrestle with constructing new concepts. Children need to be given time to dig into interesting phenomena and to revisit challenging questions.

Good assessment involves a strong commitment to child-centered learning. Curiosity, persistence, critical thinking, and communicating ideas are behaviors that indicate children are enjoying the process of learning.

Unfortunately, the joy of learning represented in the phrase, "this child loves to learn, and learns for the sake of learning" tends to become less and less the case as children progress through school and society. The challenge of sustaining the child's innate quest for knowledge is central to our mission as teachers. Our adult ways of assessing and validating the child's performance can have a powerful impact on children's lifelong learning.

The Goals of Active, Productive Assessment

- Recognize student progress and illuminate needs for future growth.

- Guide adults in stimulating and empowering each child to achieve his or her full learning potential.

Chapter 10 To Build A Bridge

Creating Early Childhood Math & Science Programs

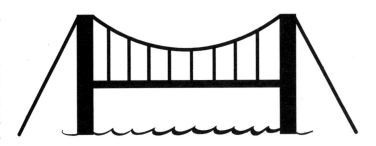

With funding from the National Science Foundation) in 1994, the PEACHES Program conducted three years of summer institutes, plus academic year sessions, for preschool and kindergarten teachers through a program called "Bridging Preschool and Kindergarten through Teacher Enhancement in Science and Mathematics." The goal was not only to improve and increase classroom science and math experiences for young children, but to improve the articulation and fitting together—the bridging—of preschool and kindergarten programs.

The participating teams were a wonderful mix of university, district, state-funded, Head Start, and private institutions. One team partnered with their city zoo, which was establishing a family program for young children.

For three weeks each summer, teachers were immersed in science and math content and teaching strategies. The program focused on how science and math education can support other key aspects of an early childhood program, including assessment, parent/family involvement, language development, equity and access for all learners, and especially the successful transition to primary school.

Since the final institute in 1996, evaluation results have been overwhelmingly positive. Teams report advances in children's learning, and an increase in inquiry-based skills, such as making observations, comparisons, recognizing cause-and-effect relationships, and applying science and math knowledge to new situations in meaningful ways.

Teams were successful in developing "bridging" activities. One preschool class was invited to a kindergarten class, not only to see what a kindergarten environment was like, but to share their terrariums and stories about snails—activities that both classes had experienced. Other teams conducted Science Nights where families took part in a bubble festival.

Leadership Role

Teams were required to take a larger leadership role at their site and provide staff and professional development experiences for their colleagues. They reported an average of 18 presentations per year for parents, teachers, and administrators. This was far beyond the three workshops they were required to do, demonstrating their dedication and the tremendous impact the project had on their own professional growth and leadership.

Close to the end of our time together at each summer institute, we shared the presentation on the following pages, which helped sum up what we had learned and discussed over the previous three weeks. We used a simple, wooden model of a bridge to gradually "build" a bridge throughout the presentation. It was a way to visually present the "bridging" that takes place among teachers, parents, and children through their experiences in science and mathematics. It was very well received and teachers were excited about using it at parent nights, teacher inservices, or administration meetings.

As with all our lessons for children, it is meant to be flexible. We hope you change it, adapt it, further develop it, and above all, find it useful for communicating the great and urgent need for effective early childhood mathematics and science programs for **all** young children.

Presenter's Notes: To Build A Bridge

Introduction

We left this presentation in outline form in the hope it will be useful for your own presentation. It is best presented by two people taking turns presenting the script as they build and label the model bridge.

1. Bridges are everywhere! Why do we need bridges? *[To get from one place to another, to help us cross over rivers, etc.]*

2. Read two short quotations from the book *Bridges* by Ken Robbins.

    "I have always been impressed by the beauty and ingenuity of bridges. To my mind they reflect everything bold, ambitious, and strong about human nature.

    "Bridges shorten our journey and ease our way. Many kinds have been built over the centuries, each suited to a special purpose and place—from a simple wooden footbridge across a quiet creek to an immense steel suspension bridge soaring high above a mile-wide river."

    — from the Author's Note

    "A log across a creek is the simplest kind of bridge. It must be long enough to reach from one bank to the other, as well as strong enough to carry the weight of a person. This simple span has just one part, the tree, though most bridges have many. Engineers call the parts members, because like members of a team they work together to make the bridge strong."

    — from page 6

3. A **bridge** connects one place with another. In a **child's educational journey**, he or she crosses many bridges. Some of the bridges children cross are when they move from one school or classroom to another, from preschool to kindergarten, from grade to grade.

4. Another bridge we want young children to cross is built through use of the **National Standards for Science and Mathematics**, as well as the National Association for the Education of Young Children (NAEYC) guidelines for **Developmentally Appropriate Practice.** This bridge is based in a science and math program grounded in these standards and held together with tools and methodology that support an effective early childhood program. This bridge will start our children on their path toward **science and mathematics literacy.**

5. There are many **people** involved in constructing and designing a bridge as well as people who help children across. It is an ongoing and challenging task.

    • Starting with the construction of the bridge, **teachers, curriculum specialists, and administrators** determine the kind of bridge needed. The bridge must have strength in content and skills, as well as be inviting to cross. Teachers help students cross this bridge by creating nurturing environments that foster hands-on, inquiry-based learning in all areas of the curriculum.

    • There are the **parents** who help their children cross bridges—including this one—and provide a supporting and guiding hand. They have **high expectations** for their children and can be embraced as partners in their children's education.

6. So how do we get started building this bridge to math and science literacy?

Building the Bridge:
The TOWERS of Big Ideas

1. To make a suspension bridge (like the Golden Gate Bridge in San Francisco) we need **TOWERS**. The towers hold up the bridge just as the **big ideas** in mathematics and science hold and structure the curriculum.

2. Let's start with a **MATHEMATICS TOWER**. The "big ideas" for preschool/K through 2nd grade come from the National Council of Teachers of Mathematics (NCTM) math standards for young children. These are the ones we consider most important.

PATTERNS

Patterns are everywhere—in nature, art, science, music, history—and they are at the heart of mathematics. A pattern can be found in anything that repeats itself over and over. Starting at a young age, children experience pattern when going about daily routines, doing activities that involve repetitive sequences (such as songs, finger-plays, rhythmic clapping), and by finding patterns in their environment. Building on these experiences, children learn to identify, analyze and extend patterns. Looking for patterns is an important problem-solving strategy, and patterns help children develop the ability to form generalizations.

NUMBER

Often young children first learn to count by rote. They need opportunities to connect numbers meaningfully in the real world. From understanding number/quantity relationships, they can learn about basic computational operations (addition, subtraction, multiplication, division), but the number strand is NOT limited to those operations. Students can move on to learn how numbers work and about the number system itself, with activities involving place value (grouping and regrouping). Gaining number sense

also involves estimation—making good guesses and being able to determine actual numbers. Number permeates all aspects of mathematics and is best understood in context. Throughout the units (in *Eggs Eggs Everywhere* and *Ladybugs* among others), number is woven into activities such as when the children identify and count insect parts.

GEOMETRY and SPATIAL SENSE

Geometry connects us to the real world—everything has a shape or form. From their earliest days, children explore shapes and structures in their environment. As their language develops, they learn the names and characteristics of two- and three-dimensional shapes. As they compare shapes, they can recognize congruent and similar shapes. They also develop spatial sense as they build, give and follow directions, navigate objects and themselves, and put things together and take them apart. In *Build It! Festival*, students identify and fill shapes, gain vocabulary, and work with congruence, symmetry, and tangrams.

MEASUREMENT

For young children, measurement begins with comparisons—which item is bigger? who has the most? what is heavier? Children love to compare themselves to everything! When they begin to measure real objects and events, nonstandard, familiar items (toothpicks, wooden cubes) can be used as a measuring tool as can non-uniform, nonstandard units of measurement (hand-spans or foot lengths). Using these tools, they learn the technique of measuring lengths and areas. Once the measurement is taken and quantified, comparisons can be made. Questions, such as "How long is each item?" "Which item is longer?" "How much longer?" can then be answered. As measurement skills and understanding grow, measuring tools can be expanded to include a standard unit of measurement such as a ruler.

STATISTICS and PROBABILITY

We're deluged with statistics in newspapers, sports, and nutritional information. We need to be able to understand the data presented to us as well as interpret it. Often decisions are made based on data. As a first step, children need opportunities to collect, organize, and describe data that has meaning to them. Graphing is one tool they can use to help them along that path. Once the data is organized, children can "read it" for the factual information it provides and, when ready, can make interpretations about it. With young children, we begin with two row (or column) concrete graphs so children can compare and make observations about a small amount of data. This is also an opportunity to use numbers in context. As children gain more experience with graphs, they can compare more items as well as record representations of concrete graphs. In *Eggs Eggs Everywhere*, students graph animals by the number of legs; in *Frog Math* students graph their hand-crafted buttons; and in *Treasure Boxes*, they graph treasure items using an open-ended graphing grid.

PROBLEM SOLVING

Problem solving involves analytic thinking and reasoning. Young children are natural problem-solvers who approach challenges with a positive attitude. In the process of solving problems, they develop strategies that can be applied to new situations. The process by which they solve problems is as important as their solutions. Students need encouragement and support in articulating the processes they use to reach solutions to problems. In addition, they need assistance identifying different problem-solving strategies to develop a "tool kit" they can use when they approach new situations.

The problems posed for young children need to have a real-world context so they have meaning and a reason to solve them for children. In addition, children should have many opportunities to solve a variety of problems that focus on different strategies. Children should see that many problems have more than one solution and evaluate which solution or solutions is best to use to solve a particular problem.

Problems that help develop mathematical content need to be embedded in the rest of the curriculum as well. For problem solving to permeate the mathematics program and other curricula, it is best nurtured in an environment that supports exchange of ideas, questioning, and investigations.

3. All of these areas of mathematics that young children work in are **interwoven** and come to life when connected with other disciplines.

4. Now let's look at a **SCIENCE TOWER.** In science there are also "big ideas" that young children need to learn. The *National Science Education Standards* outline content objectives in eight separate areas. The following four areas below are drawn from the standards: Living Things, The Environment, and Life Cycles are all part of the Life Science national standard; Physical and Earth Science is taken from the Earth and Space Science and the Physical Science national standards. These areas are the ones we consider most appropriate to emphasize with young learners.

LIVING THINGS

We know young children are curious about the natural world! They begin to ask questions about living things they see everyday. Where do birds live? What do ants eat? How fast do plants grow? They learn all living things need certain things to survive—air, water, food, shelter—and, for plants, nutrients and sunlight. In addition, children see how physical characteristics and behaviors help organisms to survive—ants have strong jaws to carry food, pill bugs roll in a ball to protect themselves.

Being good observers and asking good questions is the first step to identifying the many diverse and common characteristics of living things.

THE ENVIRONMENT

For young children, their first environment is the home. From there, they venture out into their neighborhood and school. The living environment is especially inviting for young children to explore. Both outdoors and indoors—with terrariums and aquariums—children can investigate an animal's home and habitat. They discover an animal's home provides food, water, shelter, and air. How an animal behaves is often related to its environment. A damp, cool garden of tender greens is a place where active snails would make their home. Animals, including humans, can change the environment for better or for worse. Living things and their environment are interdependent. This balance of nature is critical if all are to continue to live and prosper.

LIFE CYCLES

Cycles are important patterns in nature. Life cycles are particularly relevant to young children as they observe insects hatching from eggs, developing into adults, reproducing, and eventually dying. Growing a garden helps children see the life cycle of plants, as they plant seeds, watch them sprout, and grow to mature plants with new seeds. Along with the sequence of the cycle, children see how plants and animals look and act like their parents. Some of these characteristics are inherited and others are learned. Bears inherit their fuzzy fur from their parents but they learn from their mother how to climb a tree when in danger.

PHYSICAL and EARTH SCIENCE

Young children need plenty of opportunities to freely explore materials. They learn the "stuff" of the material world has properties they can observe—weight, shape, size, color, temperature—and it can mix and interact with other materials. In *Eggs Eggs Everywhere*, children roll, slide, and spin different objects. In other units, such as *Sifting Through Science* and *Liquid Explorations*, children explore sand and liquids to see how different materials can be mixed and separated from each other. "Messing around" with materials is a good introduction to the properties of substances and how they interact. Later on, students will explore how materials relate to sound, light, heat, electricity, and magnetism.

The CABLE:
Math & Science Processes

1. We've put up the towers with the "big ideas" in math and science. Now this bridge needs a **SUSPENSION CABLE**. This cable represents the math and science processes—the ways children look at and explore the world.

2. These processes are the basis for **SCIENTIFIC AND MATHEMATICAL INQUIRY.** Young children begin to develop inquiry skills by using these processes to ask questions, conduct an investigation, use tools to collect data, come up with explanations from the data, and communicate their findings to others.

3. The processes:

OBSERVING

Children take an active role approaching new materials and animals—carefully looking at and examining the world around them and using all their senses to observe and gather information. Simple tools such as hand lenses can be used. Use the discovery approach: don't tell children answers first, let them freely explore!

COMPARING

The next step after observing is making comparisons. How are things the same or different? Is it heavier? bigger? older? warmer? Making comparisons helps gather information about what is being observed. Children can begin to take measurements with nonstandard measurement tools to make detailed comparisons.

COMMUNICATING

As children observe and compare, they naturally talk about their findings. Working with a partner or in a small group, they discuss their observations. There are many ways to do this: sharing with one person, having a group reporter tell findings to the class, and using drama to act out the observations.

ORGANIZING

As we gather information, we need to group our data and keep track of it to make it understandable. Children often do this naturally by grouping like things and identifying characteristics. Sorting like objects or creating a graph are examples of organizing.

RECORDING

Recording is any method of putting down findings. Children can record by making a model of an animal, drawing a picture, dictating a story, keeping a journal, and acting out information in a drama. Videos and cameras are also tools we can use to record what children know.

4. These process skills support lifelong learning and inquiry—not just in the content areas of science and mathematics, but in all aspects of learning! In later grades, children will see how scientists use the same processes and methods to conduct their investigations.

5. We have a suspension cable for our bridge, but the ends are loose! What can we do about that?

The ABUTMENTS:
Tools for Implementation

1. We still need the anchors, or as they are known on bridges, the **ABUTMENTS.** The abutments in our bridge metaphor are the tools for the implementation of the math and science curriculum and process skills. They are effective early childhood teaching strategies, and are defined in the NAEYC *Guidelines for Developmentally Appropriate Practice*.

ACTIVE LEARNING

Children participate by using all their senses, and learn through doing. They take an active role rather than sitting back passively and having the teacher dispense knowledge.

CONCRETE MATERIALS

As children are actively learning, they need concrete materials with which to work and learn. Hands-on, minds-on experiences provide meaningful ways to gain understanding.

COOPERATIVE LEARNING

Children need to learn how to work together and collaborate, starting by sharing materials, and moving on to sharing knowledge, ideas, and cooperative logic and problem solving. The Fortune 500 companies cite the ability to work cooperatively and collaboratively as the most important attribute they look for in new employees.

INTEGRATED CURRICULUM

Learning needs to be in context with subject areas tied together so they have more meaning. Introduce a topic with a story. Do integrated math/science activities. Follow up with an art project or drama. Take a field trip.

REAL-WORLD SITUATIONS

Learning connected to children's lives and environment will be more interesting and meaningful to them! Pay attention to what the children bring in or ask questions about. Use these interests as a springboard for further investigations. If a child brings in a caterpillar, talk about where it came from, how to care for it, and watch it grow and change.

EQUITY & ACCESS

Make learning and content accessible to all children—girls and boys; children of all cultural backgrounds; children of all economic levels; children who are English-language learners. Use lots of visual aids and concrete materials in context to help all children have access to information despite any impediments to learning.

ASSESSMENT

As we improve our methods of teaching and instruction, so must our assessments improve. At best, assessments are a window into children's understanding of what they've explored and learned. For teachers, assessment provides checkpoints to evaluate and change curriculum to address children's progress. Some examples of authentic assessment include activity-based (performance-based) assessment, drawings, dictation, and pre- and post-assessment of knowledge (for example, have children draw a picture of an ant before and after they experience *Ant Homes Under the Ground*).

Additional CABLES: Additional Support Systems

1. There are extra cables here—what do they represent on our bridge?

2. They are additional support lines for children.

PARENT INVOLVEMENT

Parents can play an important role in the classroom assisting with activities. Studies show parent participation in schools has a dramatic impact in raising students' performance and test scores. Parents are instrumental in sharing activities, as well as their professions and experience. They serve as important role models. Have parent nights to keep them apprised of what their children are learning as well as sending letters home with updates on classroom activities.

FAMILY SUPPORT

Parent and family involvement continues at home. In the home, parents and other adult caregivers can reinforce what is learned at school and build on it. Many early childhood activities, including GEMS festivals, can be used as part of family nights, along with programs such as Family Math (from the EQUALS program at LHS). Send home an activity to connect learning at home with school (such as the young opossum measurement activity in *Mother Opossum and Her Babies*). Let children bring items from home, such as a toy bear, and use them in sorting and classifying activities.

COMMUNITY RESOURCES

Take children to libraries, museums, parks, universities, businesses, and on other field trips. Ask community organizations for help with donations, materials, and expertise. Reach out to all the diverse communities of your children and region.

The ROADWAY:
Ability To Go Back and Forth Across the Bridge

1. Finally, we need the **ROADWAY**—the last piece of the bridge. With all the supporting structures we can now put up a roadway. The roadway allows for free flow across the bridge in both directions—there is fluidity, movement, transport, and exchange.

2. Acquiring science and math literacy is a lifelong process. The child can cross over the bridge many times, taking a new piece of knowledge or applying something known to a new situation or problem. The free flow of learning allows for individual growth, development, and creativity.

Follow-Up Activity/Debriefing

1. Now that we have constructed this bridge as a metaphor for creating strong science and mathematics programs, you have a chance to build your own bridge.

   a. Distribute building materials (a variety of blocks), set a stage for building, give a time limit (10 minutes or more, depending on your circumstances), and let each group of participants start working together at a table to build a bridge.

   b. After the bridge-building activity, take a group tour of the bridges the participants built. As appropriate, discuss their similarities and differences, and the way the bridges represent the theme of diversity and unity.

2. Ask participants for their ideas about how their bridge-building connected to the bridge metaphor. What skills did they use, what big ideas did they find themselves putting into practice? What surprised them? What did they learn?

3. Conclude by saying that just as each table group constructed their own bridge, so too will participants build their own science and mathematics programs back at their schools. Each of their active science and mathematics programs will help carry students over many bridges, on the journey of exploration and investigation that is mathematics and science.

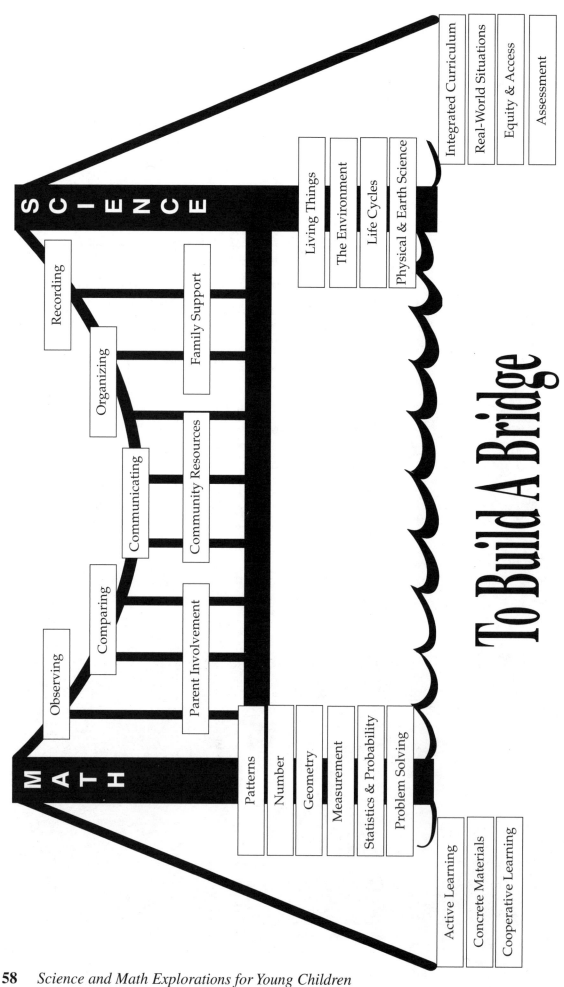

To Build A Bridge

Chapter 11 A Look to the New Millennium

This chapter is adapted from a speech given by PEACHES Director and GEMS Associate Director Kimi Hosoume in early 1999. She appeared on a special panel at the Annual National Conference of the American Association for the Advancement of Science (AAAS) to highlight achievements and future goals in early childhood education.

If I were to summarize the significant improvements in early childhood science education over the past 10 years, I would include an increased level of awareness and commitment to the following principles. These principles in turn illuminate needed future directions.

1. **Science and math for young children must be developmentally appropriate and should address and support other areas of the early childhood curriculum.**

There have been meetings among the concerned professional groups, but there needs to be more discussions and studies to clearly identify the components of **inquiry for young learners** and how this understanding can be integrated and supported by early childhood practice. The National Council of Teachers of Mathematics (NCTM) recently developed standards in math for preschool as part of their *Standards 2000* efforts.

Early childhood educational leaders and curriculum developers need to continue our collaborative work with leading scientific, mathematical, and educational organizations to further develop guidelines for preschool science and mathematics education. What kinds of programs best constitute a standards-based approach to early childhood curriculum and instruction?

2. Teachers of young children are professionals and leaders in early childhood science education reform.

They are capable and experienced at presenting strong content and skills in science and math and excel at integrating the best tenets of early learning to make the experiences appropriate, as well as content- and skill-rich. They are dedicated and committed to working with their colleagues and to sharing the strengths and value of the science/math program.

We need more opportunities for professional and staff development for early childhood educators to assist them in taking a stronger leadership role in science reform in their school, district, or regional network. We also need to expand science education efforts for daycare providers, childcare centers, and parents. I am convinced that more appropriate and powerful materials can be developed for this audience.

3. Materials should address the best teaching practices of both early childhood and science inquiry for young learners.

We need to continue the development of materials that embrace developmentally appropriate practice and emphasize an integrated curriculum approach, especially with experiences that provide for language and early literacy development.

4. Parents, family, the community are necessary active partners in children's science learning.

The past 10 years has seen a significant increase in the amount of support and interest from groups and organizations to provide more resources and extend science learning into the home and community.

We need to continue the recruitment and involvement of families at home, and of community partners such as science and children's museums and centers, to support learning in the classroom. We need to have the active and informed involvement of television and other media, technology (including developmentally appropriate and effective computer software) and Internet opportunities to provide more experiences and resources in the parent, family, and community arenas.

5. Science during the early years is a continuum of learning, and should not be compartmentalized into preschool, kindergarten, and primary school divisions.

More dialogue and communication is taking place among the teachers of these groups to make sure children are prepared for the next level of learning. Back in 1989, we named our program PEACHES (Preschool Explorations for Children and Educators in Science), but as the program developed we realized our efforts were for all young children—not just preschoolers. So, now the "P" in PEACHES stands for *Primary*, emphasizing this bridging continuum of early childhood learning.

We need more programs and materials for early childhood teachers that span and articulate the preschool through primary years to ensure strong communication and collaboration. This should result in constructing a solid foundation for children, in preparation for the high learning expectations suggested by the increased emphasis on national standards. All children should have the opportunity to take part in early childhood programs that prepare them for more advanced learning in elementary and later grades.

In Closing

It's safe to say that up until the late 1980s, the general public's perception of preschool teachers and childcare providers was too often that of "baby-sitters." Their main responsibilities were seen as taking care of and socializing children. When it came to teaching them science or mathematics, that was not considered possible! It was thought science and math were too difficult for small children to do and understand, and should be taught later in their schooling.

But the National Science Foundation, the U.S. Department of Education, AAAS, NCTM, and NAEYC were already on the way to a new understanding. They and other educational organizations across the country were well aware that research found the early years are prime for active learning of both knowledge and skills in many domains, and that science and math can play an invaluable role in that process.

Thank you for your support and recognition that young learners and their teachers can do, learn, and teach science and mathematics. We are certain that the "seeds of science" we are planting will bear fruit as the children we teach today become the citizens of tomorrow. With your ongoing support, we will continue our educational efforts into the new millennium!

NATIONAL SCIENCE EDUCATION STANDARDS
K–4

These standards are from the *National Science Education Standards* by the National Research Council. Please see the Introduction on page 12 for an explanatory note as to why we selected these five standards.

The criteria for each standard, and its relevancy to preschool–2nd grade students, is on pages 64–70.

GEMS/PEACHES GUIDES	Science as Inquiry	Science in Personal and Social Perspectives	Earth and Space Science	Life Science	Physical Science
Animal Defenses	√		√	√	
Ant Homes Under the Ground	√		√	√	√
Bubble Festival	√	√			√
Build It! Festival	√				√
Buzzing A Hive	√	√		√	√
Eggs Eggs Everywhere	√			√	√
Frog Math	√				
Group Solutions	√				
Groups Solutions, Too!	√				
Hide A Butterfly	√			√	
Investigating Artifacts	√	√		√	√
Involving Dissolving	√	√			√
Ladybugs	√	√		√	
Liquid Explorations	√	√			√
Mother Opossum and Her Babies	√			√	
Penguins and Their Young	√			√	√
Secret Formulas	√	√			√
Sifting Through Science	√	√			√
Terrarium Habitats	√	√	√	√	
Treasure Boxes	√	√			√
Tree Homes	√	√		√	

NATIONAL MATHEMATICS STANDARDS
PreK–2

These standards are from the *Principles and Standards for School Mathematics*
by the National Council of Teachers of Mathematics (NCTM). Please see the Introduction
on page 12 for an explanatory note as to why we selected these six standards.

The criteria for each standard is on pages 70–76

GEMS/PEACHES Guides	Number	Geometry and Spatial Sense	Measurement	Patterns	Statistics and Probability	Problem Solving
Animal Defenses	√	√				√
Ant Homes	√	√		√	√	√
Bubble Festival	√	√	√			√
Build It! Festival	√	√	√	√		√
Buzzing A Hive	√	√		√		√
Eggs Eggs Everywhere	√	√			√	√
Frog Math	√	√		√	√	√
Group Solutions	√					√
Groups Solutions, Too!	√	√		√	√	√
Hide A Butterfly		√				√
Investigating Artifacts	√				√	√
Involving Dissolving	√		√			√
Ladybugs	√	√		√		√
Liquid Explorations	√	√	√			√
Mother Opossum	√		√			√
Penguins	√	√	√			√
Secret Formulas	√		√	√		√
Sifting Through Science	√	√			√	√
Terrarium Habitats	√		√		√	√
Treasure Boxes	√	√			√	√
Tree Homes	√	√	√	√		√

NATIONAL SCIENCE EDUCATION STANDARDS

Science as Inquiry

All K–4 students should develop an understanding of:

Abilities Necessary to Do Scientific Inquiry

- Ask a question about objects, organisms, and events in the environment.
- Plan and conduct a simple investigation.
- Employ simple equipment and tools to gather data and extend the senses.
- Use data to construct a reasonable explanation.
- Communicate investigations and explanation.

Understandings About Scientific Inquiry

- Scientific investigations involve asking and answering a question and comparing the answer with what scientists already know about the world.
- Scientists use different kinds of investigations (such as describing objects, events, and organisms; classifying them; and doing a fair test (experimenting) depending on the questions they are trying to answer.
- Simple instruments, such as magnifiers, thermometers, and rulers, provide more information than scientists obtain using only their senses.
- Scientists develop explanations using observations (evidence) and what they already know about the world (scientific knowledge). Good explanations are based on evidence from investigations.
- Scientists make the results of their investigations public and describe them in ways that others can repeat the investigations.
- Scientists review and ask questions about the results of other scientists' work.

> **Science as Inquiry**—*for young learners*
>
> Children develop the abilities to explore their world when they practice the inquiry skills described here. These skills prepare them to later on understand scientific inquiry from a scientist's point of view and see how that process is similar and different from the ways they explore at home and school. GEMS and PEACHES emphasize inquiry skills for children in all of their units.

— GEMS/PEACHES CONNECTIONS —

Animal Defenses	Group Solutions	Mother Opossum and Her Babies
Ant Homes Under the Ground	Groups Solutions, Too!	Penguins and Their Young
Bubble Festival	Hide A Butterfly	Secret Formulas
Build It! Festival	Investigating Artifacts	Sifting Through Science
Buzzing A Hive	Involving Dissolving	Terrarium Habitats
Eggs Eggs Everywhere	Ladybugs	Treasure Boxes
Frog Math	Liquid Explorations	Tree Homes

Science in Personal and Social Perspectives

All K–4 students should develop understanding of:

Personal Health

- Safety and security are basic needs of humans. Safety involves freedom from danger, risk, or injury. Security involves feelings of confidence and lack of anxiety and fear. Student understandings include following safety rules for home and school, preventing abuse and neglect, avoiding injury, knowing whom to ask for help, and when and how to say no.

- Individuals have some responsibility for their own health. Students should engage in personal care—dental hygiene, cleanliness, and exercise—that will maintain and improve health. Understandings include how communicable diseases, such as colds, are transmitted and some of the body's defense mechanisms that prevent or overcome illness.

- Nutrition is essential to health. Students should understand how the body uses food and how various foods contribute to health. Recommendations for good nutrition include eating a variety of foods, eating less sugar, and eating less fat.

- Different substances can damage the body and how it functions. Such substances include tobacco, alcohol, over-the-counter medicines, and illicit drugs. Students should understand that some substances, such as prescription drugs, can be beneficial, but that any substance can be harmful if used inappropriately.

Characteristics and Changes in Population

- Human populations include groups of individuals living in a particular location. One important characteristic of a human population is the population density—the number of individuals of a particular population that lives in a given amount of space.

- The size of a human population can increase or decrease. Populations will increase unless other factors such as disease or famine decrease the population.

> ### Science in Personal and Social Perspectives
> *—for young learners*
>
> Even at an early age, children need to be aware of their own health, nutrition, and safety. In many GEMS and PEACHES units, children use materials such as soap and food items that, if not used safely, could cause irritation (such as getting materials in eyes or spilling on clothes). Children are encouraged to handle materials safely for the health and well-being of themselves and their classmates. Many activities involve eating and foods, and relate both to the nutrition and feeding behaviors of other animals and humans. When children explore materials they are introduced to the origin of these resources. Many units introduce the notion of conserving resources as well as emphasizing the reuse and recycling of materials.

NATIONAL SCIENCE EDUCATION STANDARDS

Science in Personal and Social Perspectives (continued)

Types of Resources
- Resources are things that we get from the living and nonliving environment to meet the needs and wants of a population.

- Some resources are basic materials, such as air, water, and soil; some are produced from basic resources, such as food, fuel, and building materials; and some resources are nonmaterial, such as quiet places, beauty, security, and safety.

- The supply of many resources is limited. If used, resources can be extended through recycling and decreased use.

Changes in Environments
- Environments are the space, conditions, and factors that affect an individual's and a population's ability to survive and their quality of life.

- Changes in environments can be natural or influenced by humans. Some changes are good, some are bad, and some are neither good nor bad. Pollution is a change in the environment that can influence the health, survival, or activities of organisms, including humans.

- Some environmental changes occur slowly, and others occur rapidly. Students should understand the different consequences of changing environments in small increments over long periods as compared with changing environments in large increments over short periods.

Science and Technology in Local Challenges
- People continue inventing new ways of doing things, solving problems, and getting work done. New ideas and inventions often affect other people; sometimes the effects are good and sometimes they are bad. It is helpful to try to determine in advance how ideas and inventions will affect other people.

- Science and technology have greatly improved food quality and quantity, transportation, health, sanitation, and communication. These benefits of science and technology are not available to all the people in the world.

— GEMS/PEACHES CONNECTIONS —

Bubble Festival	Ladybugs	Terrarium Habitats
Buzzing A Hive	Liquid Explorations	Treasure Boxes
Investigating Artifacts	Secret Formulas	Tree Homes
Involving Dissolving	Sifting Through Science	

NATIONAL SCIENCE EDUCATION STANDARDS

Earth and Space Science

All K–4 students should develop an understanding of:

Properties of Earth Materials

- Earth materials are solid rocks and soils, water, and the gases of the atmosphere. The varied materials have different physical and chemical properties, which make them useful in different ways, for example, as building materials, as sources of fuel, or for growing the plants we use as food. Earth materials provide many of the resources that humans use.

- Soils have properties of color and texture, capacity to retain water, and ability to support the growth of many kinds of plants, including those in our food supply.

> ### Earth and Space Science
> *—for young learners*
>
> Children are naturally curious about rocks and stones, soil and water. Their observations and explorations of these characteristics helps them understand how these materials help plants to grow and animals to build homes. Examining fossils and remains of animals once living, such as shells and bones, helps children understand about how animals lived and what their environment was like.

- Fossils provide evidence about the plants and animals that lived long ago and the nature of the environment at that time.

Objects in the Sky

- The sun, moon, stars, clouds, birds, and airplanes all have properties, locations, and movements that can be observed and described.

- The sun provides the light and heat necessary to maintain the temperature of the earth.

Changes in the Earth and Sky

- The surface of the earth changes. Some changes are due to slow processes, such as erosion and weathering, and some changes are due to rapid processes, such as landslides, volcanic eruptions, and earthquakes.

- Weather changes from day to day and over the seasons. Weather can be described by measurable quantities, such as temperature, wind direction and speed, and precipitation.

- Objects in the sky have patterns of movement. The sun, for example, appears to move across the sky in the same way every day, but its path changes slowly over the seasons. The moon moves across the sky on a daily basis much like the sun. The observable shape of the moon changes from day to day in a cycle that lasts about a month.

— GEMS/PEACHES CONNECTIONS —

Animal Defenses   Ant Homes Under the Ground   Terrarium Habitats

NATIONAL SCIENCE EDUCATION STANDARDS

Life Science

All K–4 students should develop understanding of:

The Characteristics of Organisms

- Organisms have basic needs. For example, animals need air, water, and food; plants require air, water, nutrients, and light. Organisms can survive only in environments in which their needs can be met. The world has many different environments, and distinct environments support the life of different types of organisms.

- Each plant or animal has different structures that serve different functions in growth, survival, and reproduction. For example, humans have distinct body structures for walking, holding, seeing, and talking.

> **Life Science**—*for young learners*
>
> Many GEMS and PEACHES units focus on the characteristics of organisms, their life stages and life cycle as well as an organisms relationship to its environment. Children are highly motivated to investigate living things and their habitats. Ongoing projects to care for animals or maintaining living habitats (terrariums and aquariums) are especially appropriate. Learning how animals and plants grow and develop helps students understand their own development, behaviors, and characteristics as they mature.

- The behavior of individual organisms is influenced by internal cues (such as hunger) and by external cues (such as a change in the environment). Humans and other organisms have senses that help them detect internal and external cues.

Life Cycle of Organisms

- Plants and animals have life cycles that include being born, developing into adults, reproducing, and eventually dying. The details of this life cycle are different for different organisms.

- Plants and animals closely resemble their parents.

- Many characteristics of an organism are inherited from the parents of the organism, but other characteristics result from an individual's interactions with the environment. Inherited characteristics include the color of flowers and the number of limbs of an animal. Other features, such as the ability to ride a bicycle, are learned through interactions with the environment and cannot be passed on to the next generation.

Organisms and Their Environments

- All animals depend on plants. Some animals eat plants for food. Other animals eat animals that eat the plants.

- An organism's patterns of behavior are related to the nature of that organism's environment, including the kinds and numbers of other organisms present, the availability of food and resources, and the physical characteristics of the environment. When the environment changes, some plants and animals survive and reproduce, and others die or move to new locations.

- All organisms cause changes in the environment where they live. Some of these changes are detrimental to the organism or other organisms, whereas others are beneficial.

- Humans depend on their natural and constructed environments. Humans change environments in ways that can be either beneficial or detrimental for themselves and other organisms.

— GEMS/PEACHES CONNECTIONS —

Animal Defenses

Ant Homes Under the Ground

Buzzing A Hive

Eggs Eggs Everywhere

Hide A Butterfly

Investigating Artifacts

Ladybugs

Mother Opossum and Her Babies

Penguins and Their Young

Terrarium Habitats

Tree Homes

NATIONAL SCIENCE EDUCATION STANDARDS

Physical Science

All K–4 students should develop an understanding of:

Properties of Objects and Materials

- Objects have many observable properties, including size, weight, shape, color, temperature, and the ability to react with other substances. Those properties can be measured using tools.

- Objects are made of one or more materials, such as paper, wood, and metal. Objects can be described by the properties of the materials from which they are made, and those properties can be used to separate or sort a group of objects or materials.

- Materials can exist in different states-—solid, liquid, and gas. Some common materials, such as water, can be changed from one state to another by heating or cooling.

Position and Motion of Objects

- The position of an object can be described by locating it relative to another object or the background.

- An object's motion can be described by tracing and measuring its position over time.

- The position and motion of objects can be changed by pushing or pulling. The size of the change is related to the strength of the push or pull.

- Sound is produced by vibrating objects. The pitch of the sound can be varied by changing the rate of vibration.

Light, Heat, Electricity, and Magnetism

- Light travels in a straight line until it strikes an object. Light can be reflected by a mirror, refracted by a lens, or absorbed by an object.

- Heat can be produced in many ways, such as burning, rubbing, or mixing one substance with another. Heat can move from one object to another by conduction.

- Electricity in circuits can produce light, heat, sound, and magnetic effects. Electrical circuits require a complete loop through which an electrical current can pass.

- Magnets attract and repel each other and certain kinds of other materials.

> **Physical Science**—*for young learners*
>
> When children explore things in their surroundings, they discover many properties of objects—size, shape, and color, for example. Objects are made of different materials such as wood or metal, and feel and react differently when handled. They learn that there are solids and liquids, and that water can freeze and become a solid. When building with blocks or rolling objects, children observe how objects can be balanced, stacked, pushed and pulled, and that many things make sounds. These early explorations help them later on when they investigate the nature of light, heat, electricity, and magnetism.

— GEMS/PEACHES CONNECTIONS —

Ant Homes Under the Ground	Buzzing A Hive	Involving Dissolving	Secret Formulas
Bubble Festival	Eggs Eggs Everywhere	Liquid Explorations	Sifting Through Science
Build It! Festival	Investigating Artifacts	Penguins and Their Young	Terrarium Habitats
			Treasure Boxes

NATIONAL MATHEMATICS STANDARDS

Number

All PreK–2 students should understand:

Number, Ways of Representing Numbers, Relationships Among Numbers and Number Systems

- Count fluently with understanding and recognize "how many" in small sets of objects.
- Understand cardinal and ordinal meaning of numbers in quantifying, measuring, and identifying the order of objects.
- Connect number words, the quantities they represent, numerals, and written words and represent numerical situations with each of these.
- Develop an understanding of the relative magnitude of numbers and make connections between the size of cardinal numbers and the counting sequence.
- Develop an understanding of the multiple relationships among whole numbers by comparing, ordering, estimating, composing, decomposing, and grouping number, including beginning understandings of place value.
- Understand and represent familiar fractions, such as ½ and ¾.

Meaning of Operations and How They Relate to Each Other

- Understand different meanings of addition and subtraction of whole numbers and the relation between the two operations.
- Understand situations that led to multiplication and division, such as equal groupings of objects and sharing equally.
- Develop understanding about the effects of the operations on whole numbers.

Use Computational Tools and Strategies Fluently and Estimate Appropriately

- Develop and use strategies and algorithms to solve number problems.
- Develop fluency with addition and subtraction facts by the end of the second grade.
- Compute using a variety of methods, including mental computation, paper and pencil, and calculators and chose an appropriate method for the situation.
- Recognize whether numerical solutions are reasonable.

— GEMS/PEACHES CONNECTIONS —

Animal Defenses	Frog Math	Mother Opossum and Her Babies
Ant Homes Under the Ground	Group Solutions	Penguins and Their Young
Bubble Festival	Groups Solutions, Too!	Secret Formulas
Build It! Festival	Investigating Artifacts	Sifting Through Science
Buzzing A Hive	Involving Dissolving	Terrarium Habitats
Eggs Eggs Everywhere	Ladybugs	Treasure Boxes
	Liquid Explorations	Tree Homes

NATIONAL MATHEMATICS STANDARDS

Geometry and Spatial Sense

All PreK–2 students should:

Analyze Characteristics and Properties of Two- and Three-Dimensional Geometric Objects

- Recognize, name, build, draw, describe, compare, and sort two- and three-dimensional shapes.
- Recognize and locate geometric shapes and structures in the world.
- Describe attributes and parts of two- and three dimensional shapes.
- Investigate and predict results of putting together and taking apart shapes.
- Recognize congruent and similar shapes.
- Relate geometric ideas to number and measurement ideas.

Select and Use Different Representational Systems, Including Coordinate Geometry and Graph Theory

- Describe, name, interpret, and apply ideas of relative position in space.
- Describe, name, interpret, and apply ideas of direction and distance in navigating space.
- Find and name locations with simple relations (e.g. near to) and coordinate systems (maps).

Recognize the Usefulness of Transformations and Symmetry in Analyzing Mathematical Situations

- Recognize and apply slides, flips, turns; predict the effects of transformations on shapes.
- Recognize and create reflectional and rotational symmetry of two- and three-dimensional objects.

Use Visualization and Spatial Reasoning to Solve Problems Both Within and Outside Math

- Create mental images of geometric shapes (spatial memory and spatial visualization).
- Determine and represent objects from different perspectives and points of view.
- Recognize and describe spatial relationships.

— GEMS/PEACHES CONNECTIONS —

Animal Defenses	Eggs Eggs Everywhere	Liquid Explorations
Ant Homes Under the Ground	Frog Math	Penguins and Their Young
Bubble Festival	Groups Solutions, Too!	Sifting Through Science
Build It! Festival	Hide A Butterfly	Treasure Boxes
Buzzing A Hive	Ladybugs	Tree Homes

NATIONAL MATHEMATICS STANDARDS

Measurement

All PreK-2 students should:

Understand Attributes, Units, and Systems of Measurement

- Recognize the attributes of length, capacity, weight, area and time.
- Compare and order objects qualitatively by these attributes.
- Make and use measurements in natural situations.
- Develop referents for estimation.
- Develop a sense of the unit (e.g. length, area) through estimation.

Apply a Variety of Techniques, Tools, and Formulas for Determining Measurements

- Use tools, such as rulers, to measure.
- Measure with same size unit (nonstandard and standard).
- Use repetition of units (iteration) to measure length and area.

— GEMS/PEACHES CONNECTIONS —

Bubble Festival	Liquid Explorations	Secret Formulas
Build It! Festival	Mother Opossum and Her Babies	Terrarium Habitats
Involving Dissolving	Penguins and Their Young	Tree Homes

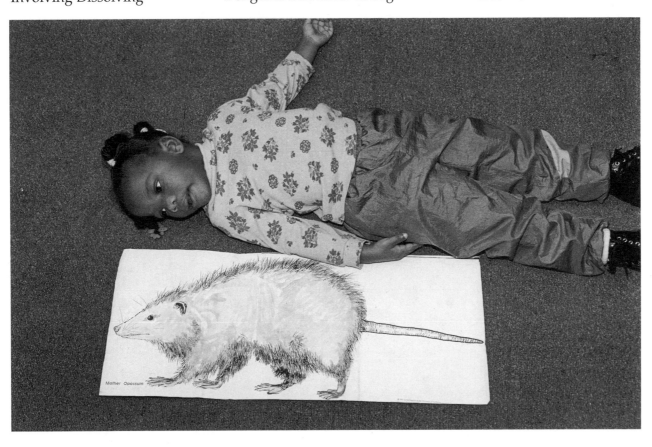

NATIONAL MATHEMATICS STANDARDS

Patterns

All PreK–2 students should:

Understand Various Types of Patterns and Functional Relationships

- Sort and classify objects by different properties.
- Order objects by size or other numerical property (seriation).
- Identify, analyze, and extend patterns and recognize the same pattern in different manifestations.
- Describe how both repeating and growing patterns are generated.

Use Symbolic Forms to Represent and Analyze Mathematical Situations and Structures

- Illustrate general principles (e.g. commutativity) using specific numbers.
- Understand reversal of operation.
- Use concrete, pictorial, and verbal representations of numerical situations, including invented notation.
- Use appropriate symbolic representation of mathematical situations.

Use Mathematical Models and Analyze Change in Both Real and Abstract Contexts

- Make comparisons and describe change qualitatively (e.g. taller than).
- Make comparisons and describe change quantitatively (e.g. 3 inches taller).
- Model concrete situations using addition and subtraction of whole numbers.

— GEMS/PEACHES CONNECTIONS —

Ant Homes Under the Ground

Build It! Festival

Buzzing A Hive

Frog Math

Groups Solutions, Too!

Ladybugs

Secret Formulas

Tree Homes

NATIONAL MATHEMATICS STANDARDS

Statistics and Probability

All PreK–2 students should:

Pose questions and collect, organize, and represent data to answer those questions

- Gather data about themselves and their surroundings to answer questions that involve multiple responses.
- Sort and classify objects and organize data according to attributes of the objects.
- Represent data to convey results at a glance using concrete objects, pictures, and numbers.

Interpret data using methods of exploratory analysis

- Describe parts of the data and data as a whole.
- Identify parts of the data with special characteristics, for example, the category with most frequent response.

Develop and evaluate inferences, predictions, and arguments that are based on data

Understand and apply basic notions of chance and probability

- Understand notions such as certain, impossible, more likely, less likely.

— GEMS/PEACHES CONNECTIONS —

Ant Homes Under the Ground

Eggs Eggs Everywhere

Frog Math

Group Solutions, Too!

Investigating Artifacts

Sifting Through Science

Terrarium Habitats

Treasure Boxes

NATIONAL MATHEMATICS STANDARDS

Problem Solving

All PreK–2 students should:

Build New Mathematical Knowledge Through Their Work With Problems

Develop a Disposition to Formulate, Represent, Abstract, and Generalize Situations Within and Without Mathematics

Apply a Wide Variety of Strategies to Solve Problems and Adapt the Strategies to New Situations

Monitor and Reflect on Their Mathematical Thinking in Solving Problems

— GEMS/PEACHES CONNECTIONS —

Animal Defenses	Group Solutions	Mother Opossum and Her Babies
Ant Homes Under the Ground	Groups Solutions, Too!	Penguins and Their Young
Bubble Festival	Hide A Butterfly	Secret Formulas
Build It! Festival	Investigating Artifacts	Sifting Through Science
Buzzing A Hive	Involving Dissolving	Terrarium Habitats
Eggs Eggs Everywhere	Ladybugs	Treasure Boxes
Frog Math	Liquid Explorations	Tree Homes

References

Abruscato, J. *Teaching Children Science*, third edition, Allyn & Bacon, Boston, 1992.

American Association for the Advancement of Science (AAAS). *Benchmarks For Science Literacy*, AAAS, Project 2061, Washington, D.C., 1993.

American Association for the Advancement of Science (AAAS). *Dialogue on Early Childhood Science, Mathematics, and Technology Education*, AAAS, Project 2061, Washington, D.C., 1999.

Armstrong, Thomas. *7 Kinds of Smart: Discovering and Using Your Natural Intelligence*, Plume/Penguin, New York, 1993.

Armstrong, Thomas. *Multiple Intelligences in the Classroom*, Association for Supervision and Curriculum Development, Alexandria, Virginia, 1994.

Armstrong, Thomas. *In Their Own Way: Discovering and Encouraging Your Child's Personal Learning Style*, Jeremy P. Tarcher Publishers, Los Angeles, 1987.

Atkin, J. Myron and Karplus, Robert, "Discovery or Invention?" *The Science Teacher*, National Science Teachers Association, Washington, D.C., 1962.

Barber, Jacqueline, et. al, *Insights and Outcomes: Assessments for Great Explorations in Math and Science*, Lawrence Hall of Science, Berkeley, California, 1995.

Begley, S. (1996, February 19). "Your Child's Brain." *Newsweek*, 55-61.

Berk, Laura E., Winsler, Adam. *Scaffolding Children's Learning: Vygotsky and Early Childhood Education*, National Association for the Education of Young Children, Washington, D.C., 1995.

Boyles, N. S. and Contadino, D. *The Learning Difference Sourcebook.* Lowell House, Los Angeles, 1997.

Bredekamp, Sue and Copple, Carol. *Developmentally Appropriate Practice in Early Childhood Programs* (revised edition), National Association for the Education of Young Children, Washington, D.C., 1997.

Bredekamp, Sue and Rosegrant, Teresa. *Reaching Potentials: Transforming Early Childhood Curriculum and Assessment*, Volume 2, National Association for the Education of Young Children, Washington, D.C., 1995.

Chang, H. N. et. al. *Looking In, Looking Out: Redefining Child Care and Early Education in a Diverse Society.* A California Tomorrow Publication, San Francisco, 1996.

Charlesworth, R., Lind, Karen K. *Math and Science for Young Children*, second edition, Delmar Publishers, Albany, New York, 1995.

Cost, Quality, and Child Outcome Study Team, *Cost, quality, and child outcomes in child care centers public report*, Economics Department, University of Colorado, Denver, 1995.

Delpit, L. *Other People's Children: Cultural Conflict in the Classroom.* The New Press., New York, 1995.

Galinsky, Ellen, et. al. *The Study of Children in Family Day Care and Relative Care*, The Families and Work Institute, New York, 1994.

Galinsky, Ellen. "New Research on the Brain Development of Young Children: Implications for Families, Early Education and Care," *Connections*, California Association for the Education of Young Children, Volume 26, Number 2, Winter Issue, 1997.

Garcia, E. E. "The Education of Hispanics in Early Childhood: Of Roots and Wings." *Young Children*, March 1997, 5-14.

Gardner, H., "Reflections on Multiple Intelligences: Myths and Messages," *Phi Delta Kappan*, November, 1995.

Gardner, Howard. *Frames of Mind: The Theory of Multiple Intelligences.* Basic Books, New York, 1983.

Gardner, H., *Multiple Intelligences: The Theory in Practice.* Basic Books, New York, 1993.

Gardner, H., *The Unschooled Mind: How Children Think and How Schools Should Teach,* HarperCollins, New York, 1992.

Genishi, Celia (editor). *Ways of Assessing Children and Curriculum: Stories of Early Childhood Practice*, Teachers College Press, Teachers College, Columbia University, New York and London, 1992.

Halford, J. M. "A Different Mirror: A Conversation with Ronald Takaki." *Educational Leadership*, April 1999, 8-13.

Harlen, W. *The Teaching of Science in Primary Schools.* (Second Edition) David Fulton Publishers, London, 1996.

Harlan, Wynne (editor). *Primary Science...Taking the Plunge, How to teach primary science more effectively,* Heinemann Educational, Oxford, 1985.

Holt, Bess-Gene. *Science with Young Children*, National Association for the Education of Young Children, Washington, D.C., 1989.

Kagan, S.L. and Cohen, N.E. *Solving the Quality Problem: A Vision for America's Early Care and Education System. A Final Report of the Quality 2000 Initiative,* Yale University, New Haven, 1997.

Kamii, Constance (editor). *Achievement Testing in the Early Grades: The Games Grown-Ups Play,* National Association for the Education of Young Children, Washington D.C., 1990.

Kober, Nancy. *EdTalk, What We Know About Science Teaching and Learning,* Council for Educational Development and Research, Washington, DC., 1992.

Ladson-Billings, Gloria. *The Dreamkeepers.* Jossey-Bass Publishers, San Francisco, 1994.

Lind, Karen K. *Exploring Science in Early Childhood: A Developmental Approach,* second edition, Delmar Publishers, Albany, New York, 1996.

Love, J.M., Schochet, P.Z., and Meckstrom, A. "Are they in any real danger? What research does—and doesn't—tell us about child care quality and children's well-being." *Mathematica Policy Research*, Princeton, New Jersey, 1996.

Love, John M., "Quality in Child Care Centers," *Early Childhood Research and Policy Briefs*, National Center for Early Development and Learning, Volume 1, Number 1, Summer 1997.

Lowery, Lawrence (editor). *NSTA Pathways to the Science Standards: Guidelines for Moving the Vision into Practice,* Elementary School Edition, National Science Teachers Association (NSTA), Arlington, Virginia, 1997.

Lowery, Lawrence. "How New Science Curriculums Reflect Brain Research." *Educational Leadership*, Association for Supervision and Curriculum Development, Volume 56, Number 3, November, 1998.

Mallory, B. L. and New, R. S. (editors). *Diversity & Developmentally Appropriate Practices: Challenges for Early Childhood Education.* Teachers College Press, New York, 1994.

Markova, D. *How Your Child Is Smart: A Life Changing Approach to Learning.* Conari Press, Berkeley, California, 1992.

McIntyre, Margaret. *Early Childhood and Science*, National Science Teachers Association, Washington D.C., 1984.

National Association for the Education of Young Children. "NAEYC Position Statement: Responding to Lingustic and Cultural Diversity-Recommendations for Effective Early Childhood Education." *Young Children,* January 1996, 4-12

National Council of Teachers of Mathematics, *Curriculum Evaluation Standards for School Mathematics,* Reston, Virginia, 1989.

National Council of Teachers of Mathematics. *Principles and Standards for School Mathematics: Standards 2000: Discussion Draft*, Reston, Virginia, 1998.

National Research Council. *National Science Education Standards*, National Academy Press, Washington D.C., 1996.

Newberger, J. J. "New Brain Research—A Window of Opportunity to Build Public Support for Early Childhood Education." *Young Children,* May 1997, 4-9.

NICHD Early Childhood Research Network. "Mother-child interaction and cognitive outcomes associated with early child care: results of the ICHD Study." Poster symposium presented at the Biennial Meeting of the Society for Research in Child Development, Washington, D.C., 1997.

Phillips, Deborah A. (editor). *Quality in Child Care: What Does Research Tell Us?* National Association for the Education of Young Children, Washington, D.C., 1993.

Project 2061, American Association for the Advancement of Science. *Science For All Americans,* Oxford University Press, New York, 1990.

Robbins, Ken. *Bridges,* Dial, New York, 1991.

Shore, Rima. *Rethinking the Brain: New Insights into Early Development,* Families and Work Institute, New York, 1997.

Tabor, P. O. *One Child, Two Languages: A Guide for Preschool Educators of Children Learning English As a Second Language.* Paul H. Brookes Publishing, Baltimore, Maryland, 1997.

Trentacosta, Janet and Kenney, Margaret J., *Multicultural and Gender Equity in the Mathematics Classroom: The Gift of Diversity*, National Council of Teachers of Mathematics, Reston, Virginia, 1997.

Whitebook, M., Howes, C., Phillips, D. *Who cares? Child care teachers and the quality of care in America: Final report, National Child Care Staffing Study*, Child Care Employee Project, Berkeley, California, 1989.

Resources Related to Questions

Here are a number of excellent books and articles that explore the impact of questions for guiding children's learning and investigations.

Harlen, W. *The Teaching of Science in Primary Schools*, second edition David Fulton Publishers, London, 1996.

> Wynne Harlen devotes several chapters of this book to the important subject of questions. She weaves information from research with powerful examples from classrooms to create practical guidelines for improving one's use of questions to stimulate and guide student learning.

Lowery, L. *Asking Effective Questions*, National Science Teachers Regional Convention, Denver, 1997.

Lowery, L. *Toward Effective Teaching: Questioning and Response Strategies*. Full Option Science System (FOSS) Monograph, 1999.

> Here are various examples of how the wise use of questions and statements affect the thinking of students. He describes three categories of questions (Narrow, Broad, and Non-instructional) and provides strategies for using the different kinds of questions effectively. For example, Broad Open-ended Questions encourage students to hypothesize, predict, and organize ideas in new ways.

Elstgeest, J. "The right question at the right time." In Harlen, W., *Primary Science: Taking the Plunge*, Heinemann Educational Books, London, 1985.

> Jos Elstgeest defines a good question as "a stimulating question which is an invitation to a closer look, a new experiment or a fresh exercise. The right question leads to where the answer can be found: to the real objects or events under study, there where the solution lies hidden." He gives examples of how to use the following kinds of questions to stimulate inquiry: Attention-focusing; Measuring; Comparison; Action, or What happens if . . . ?; and problem-posing questions.

Elstgeest, J. "Encounter, interaction, dialogue" and Jelly, S.J. "Helping children to raise questions—and answering them," both also in Harlen, W., *Primary Science: Taking the Plunge*, Heinemann Educational Books, London, 1985.

Rowe, Mary Budd, (editor). *The Process of Knowing*. Vol. 6 of *What Research Says to the Science Teacher*. National Science Teacher Association, Washington, D.C., 1990.